Gives an absolutely spot-on sense of rural life in [...]nging Transylvania, with cutting insights and a wry sense of [...]

[...] Guide to Romania

The moder[...] and inside out. Mike Ormsb[...] ransition. With an ear for lo[...] Gypsies – and a quirky eye [...] o sigh for the old days, and [...] ern world has wreaked in the [...]

[...], Author, *Along The Enchanted Way*

This isn't your usual sentimental year-in-the-sticks-abroad book. Ormsby knows Romania and writes with an insider's knowledge. Poignant, immediate, always original, he is the perfect guide to this entrancing country's strange social rituals. Romania is as fortunate to have found him as he is to have made a life there.

Robin Ashenden, *Central and Eastern European London Review*

Mike Ormsby addresses the challenges, absurdities, and everyday drama of life in rural Romania with a deep and sincere understanding. His wit and humour are alive and kicking, coupled with a zeal for storytelling, a poetic sense of what is right, and a profound respect for people he meets.

Colin Shaw, Founder & Tour Guide, *www.roving-romania.co.uk*

Domnul Mike has done it again, writing yet another book that we wished that we had written ourselves. His gift appears to be his unbounded willingness to talk to people, find things out and deal with any situation he finds himself in, no matter how ridiculous. Sublime.

Craig Turp, Editor, *Bucharest in Your Pocket*

An excellent blend of dialogue, wit, and subtle irony. These lovely stories invite us to ponder the clash of nature and culture, town and countryside, old and new beliefs and social practices, in present-day southern Transylvania.

Dr. Gabriela Colipca-Ciobanu, Associate Professor, Dunărea de Jos University

A truly enchanting read, giftedly written with ironic humour.

Christian Ivanes, Book Editor, University of Agricultural Sciences and Veterinary Medicine of Cluj-Napoca

Thanks to the author's healthy sense of humour, I read this with a smile. Welcome to *Culmea*: life is simple yet complicated, no traffic jams, no city noise, you know your neighbours, and stray dogs find homes. I enjoyed it all, even the tough bits.

Alina Vancia, News Presenter, Digi FM

© 2017, Mike Ormsby 🐦 *Ormsbymike* 🔖 *mikeormsby.net*
© 2017, Nicoaro Books 🐦 *NicoaroBooks* 🔖 *nicoarobooks.com*

All rights reserved. No part of this publication may be reproduced, or transmitted in any form or by any means, electronic or otherwise, without written permission from the author.

ISBN print edition: 978-606-93902-7-6
ISBN create space edition: 978-1973896142

Cover design by Sorin Sorasan 🔖 *sorinsorasan.com*
DTP by Victor Jalbă-Șoimaru 🔖 *prodtp.ro*
Author photo by Cosmin Bumbuț

Descrierea CIP a Bibliotecii Naționale a României
ORMSBY, MIKE
Never mind the vampires, here's Transylvania /
Mike Ormsby. – București: Nicoaro Books, 2017
ISBN: 978-606-93902-7-6

821.111

NEVER MIND THE VAMPIRES HERE'S TRANSYLVANIA

MIKE ORMSBY

Nicoaro Books
Stretch Your Mind

Table of Contents

Acknowledgements 9

The Lovely Linda 17
Red in Tooth and Claw 31
Stretch your Mind 35
Kissed by the Blade 39
Dog Willing..50
Bewitched 61
Trei Mușchetari 66
King of the Mountain 71
How to Build a Fence 99
Oh, What Fun 112
Carollateral Damage...125
The Enemy Within 133
English for Beginners...143
Titus & Iacob 151
Stretch Your Body 162
Gorgeous Music 169
Heavens Above..184
Asta e...188
Every Picture...198
Bright Spark 203
Remember Maya 209
Local Customs 221
Floating Voter 227
Yes Uke Can 230

Author Bio..235

These stories may contain nuts

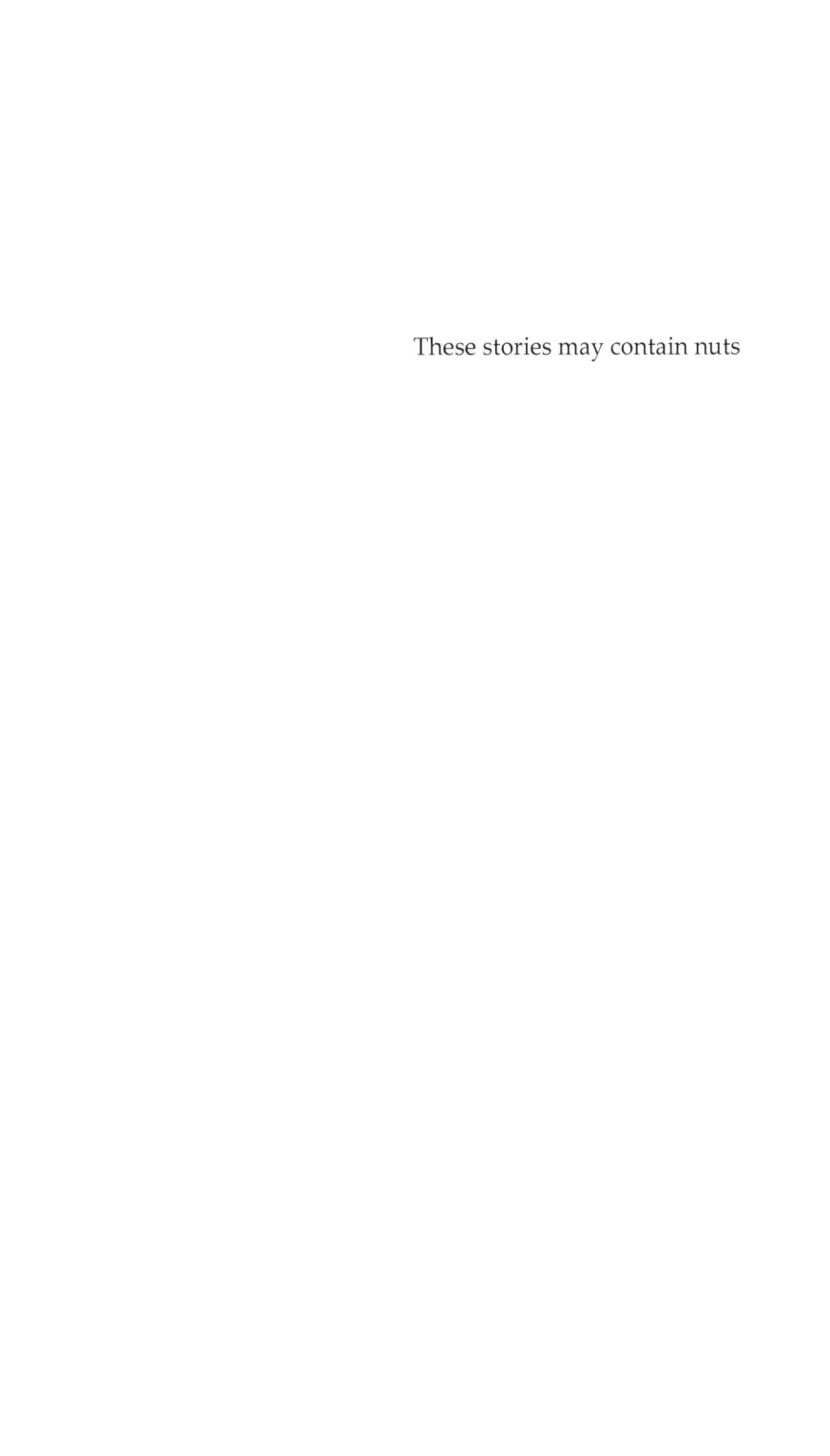

Acknowledgements

Thank you, Angela Nicoară, for editing and insight.

Thank you, Emanuela Jalbă-Șoimaru and Carmen Stanilă, for proofreading. Typos are inevitable, but I'm eternally grapefruit.

Thank you, friends and neighbours in Transylvania, Romania, for sharing your wit, wisdom, and palinca.

Mike Ormsby
Transylvania
7.7.17

For Romanians and Romaniaphiles everywhere

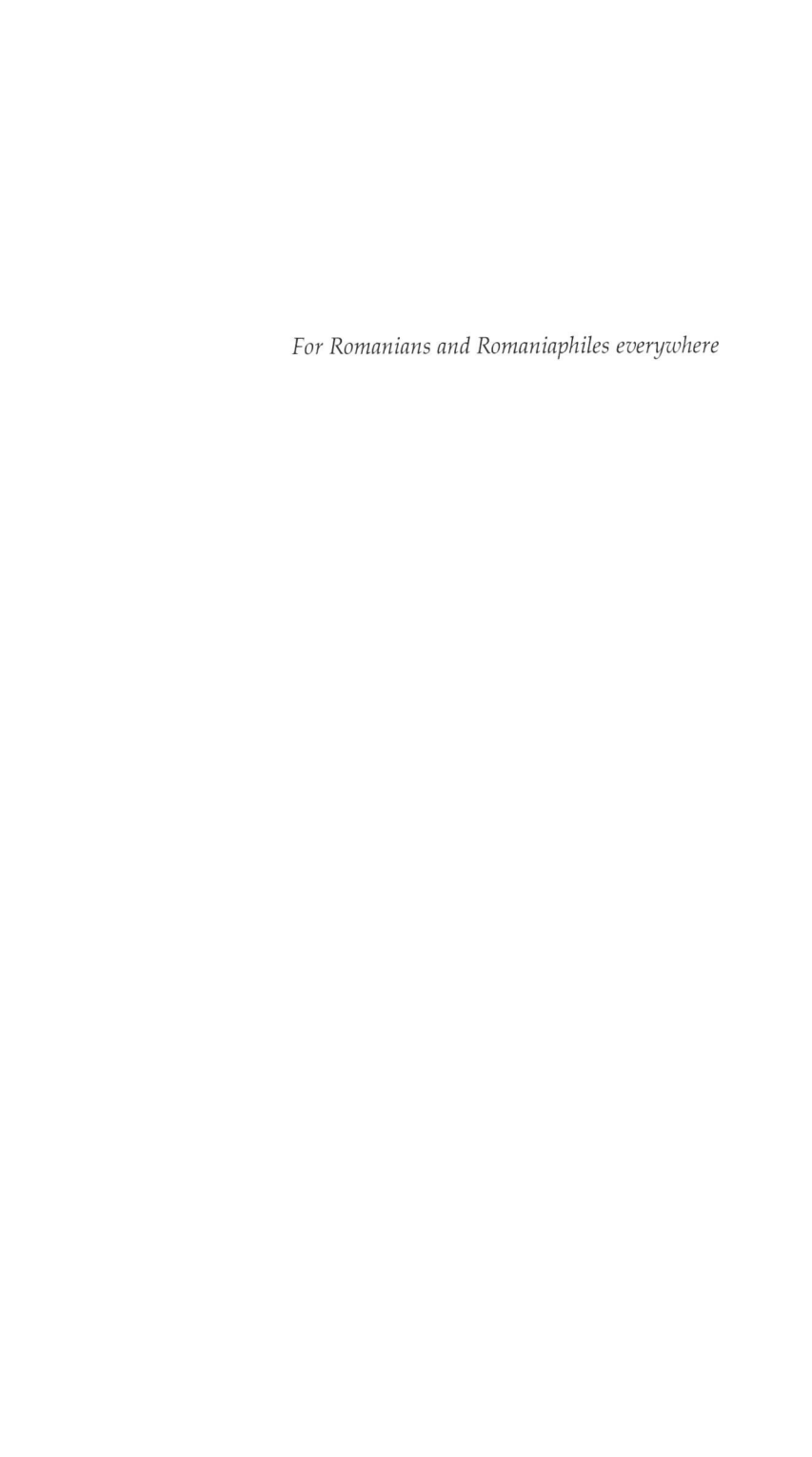

for thou hast pined
And hunger'd after Nature, many a year,
In the great City pent

S.T. Coleridge

Transylvania is located in central Romania.

The region is known for its beautiful
rural landscapes and rich history.

Transylvania is often associated with vampires,
but don't let that worry you.

The Lovely Linda

"You're back with us in Bucharest, Domnul Mike?" The cleaning lady waddles towards me in the lobby of the apartment block, pushing her trolley of buckets and brushes. Her flip-flops slap a welcome on the tiles as she approaches. "Did you press the button for the lift?"

"Yes, Doamna Tina, it should be here soon. How are you?"

"Not bad, thanks for asking. How's Doamna Angela?"

"Fine, thanks. She's upstairs in our flat."

We step into the lift and Tina pokes the control panel. She looks tired and much older than the last time we met. *Just over four years ago?* Her hands are pale, almost transparent. Must be all those buckets of soapy water. She reaches out to steady a nervous mop.

"So, where are you these days, Domnul Mike?"

"Azerbaijan, until last week. We just moved back to Romania. How are things in the block?"

"Same as ever, here."

We rise through the floors and an awkward silence descends. Nothing like a small elevator for accentuating big differences. I stare at the stainless steel door and spot a familiar graffito gouged into it: *Suck me, Vlaicu.*

It's still here after all these years. So much for our esteemed Administrator, but that's democracy, I suppose.

"How long are you two staying in Bucharest?" says Tina.

"Not long, we're moving to Transylvania. Bought a house."

"Oh, I see. So, that means you'll have a garden?"

"Quite a big one."

"Then why not take Linda?"

"Linda who?"

"Linda who lives in the car park."

"I beg your pardon?"

"Linda's a dog. Look." Tina pulls out her scuffed Nokia and shows me a photo of a scary dog with a black face and stern gaze. "She's a beauty, Domnul. See how alert! Make a good guard dog. Her dad was a Rottweiler. You'll need a dog. Do you have one?"

"No, although we are thinking about it. I want a local sheepdog, a *Ciobănesc* with a thick coat for the cold winters."

"You should take Linda, everybody here loves her."

"In that case, why has nobody here adopted her?"

"Linda's too big for these little flats, she needs to be outside."

The bell pings and the elevator doors slide apart. Tina spots Angela stacking cardboard boxes in the corridor beyond and steps out with me. She gives my wife a welcoming hug and tells her about lovely Linda who lives in the car park and why we must adopt her.

Angela checks the photo. "Linda looks a bit fierce, Tina."

"Doamna Angela, trust me, she's a lovely dog. I'll take you to meet her if you like. But the sooner the better." Tina sounds sad.

"How do you mean?" says Angela.

"The dogcatchers took her. They'll kill her, any day now."

"Kill Linda?"

"At the compound, it's what they do. Won't you save her?"

Angela looks at me and we know the answer. *Bang goes my sheepdog.*

"Are you free to visit the compound tomorrow?" says Angela.

Tina wipes tearful eyes on a sleeve. "I'll take time off."

"Great, thanks, Tina. We'll go by taxi. Say, 9 a.m.?"

"Actually, I know a lady who might drive us."

"Even better."

Nine sharp, Tina is waiting for us in the car park, dressed in a long grey anorak over a summer frock and red sandals. A skinny blonde stands nearby smoking a long cigarette and wearing a black trouser suit, black beret, silky green scarf, and big sunglasses. She looks French, as in *Résistance*. What she doesn't look is happy. Tina introduces her. "This is my friend Madeleine. She'll drive us to the dog pound."

Turns out *La Madeleine* lives in the next block, loves animals, and has rescued six street cats, some of whom appear to have slept on her beret. She jangles car keys above her head. "Borrowed some wheels. Shall we?" She beckons us and we obey, somewhat intrigued.

"Catchers can be such horrible people," says Madeleine, striding on. "They just grab any dog they can, doesn't matter what you say. I also rescued four terriers from this car park. They live on my land outside

Bucharest. I would take Linda but she's too big. I hope she's still alive. I dread going to the compound, it's terribly upsetting, I usually cry my eyes out. But any friend of Tina's is a friend of mine." She glances at the sky and frowns. "Looks like rain. Here's the car. Hop in."

The first raindrops patter down as Angela and I squeeze into a white Dacia. It's nice to be rescued. *A good omen?*

Madeleine removes her sunglasses and looks at us in the rear-view mirror. Her green eyes match her scarf, très chic.

"Listen up, guys. I can't promise anything except that we'll try, ок? Linda's quite nice-looking, so chances are she's still alive."

"They don't euthanize nice-looking dogs?" says Angela.

Madeleine smiles at us for the first time. "No, they sell 'em, even though adoptions are supposed to be free. Let's go!"

She's a good driver – not too fast, not too slow, checking her mirrors and keeping her distance. The rain is torrential and our windows are all foggy.

The dog pound consists of a few single-storey concrete buildings and a big yard behind a steel fence. We park nearby but remain in the car, waiting for the rain to ease off. We should've brought umbrellas.

"Mind if I smoke?" says Madeleine.

"Yes," says Tina.

"Shall we phone and say we've come for Linda?" says Angela.

"No point," says Madeleine, "they won't have a clue who you mean, they have far too many dogs."

"Not like Linda, they don't," says Tina. "She's lovely, she's not some mutt, like that one." Tina points at some mutt in the yard.

"Lovely unless you're a cat," says Madeleine. "Linda hates cats."

Angela glances at me. "Hear that? Linda hates cats."

"I heard. We should get a puppy instead. Sheepdog puppy."

Madeleine looks at us in the mirror. "Is there a problem?"

"Yes, we have four cats in our flat, back at the block."

"Since when did you have cats in your flat?" says Tina.

"We brought them last week from Azerbaijan, we rescued them a while ago."

Madeleine stares at Tina. *"Four cats?* You didn't say they had cats. I'm wasting my time. They can't adopt Linda, she'll eat the lot."

"I never saw Linda eat one, she just chases them," says Tina.

I lean forward. "Tina, if Linda hates cats we can't adopt her."

"She doesn't hate them, she just chases them for fun."

"It's not fun if you're a cat. What if she catches one of ours?"

"I never saw her catch one. They usually run up trees and hiss."

"We don't have trees in our apartment."

"But you're moving to Transylvania. *Quite a big garden,* you said. Oh, look, the rain's stopping. We can go and find Linda."

I sit back, wondering whether to stay put. Tina the cleaner would make a good chess player, I reckon, always one move ahead. And she's right about the rain – the deluge is drying up, just a few silver plops bouncing here and there. But she's wrong if she thinks we're adopting a cat killer.

Madeleine opens her door. "Whatever, let's try while we can."

"Well, Mike?" says Angela.

I shrug my shoulders. *Whatever.* We exit the car and follow our guides, dodging wisps of cigarette smoke. The sky rumbles, sunshine cracks a cloud, and puddles shimmer petrol blue.

Inside the main building, we stand around waiting to speak to a burly official behind the counter. He has a bushy, grey beard and horn-rimmed spectacles. He's barking into a phone. Perhaps he's worked here too long. We look at maps of Bucharest pinned on a wall. Coloured bits show where the dogcatchers have been, and when. Tina points to Sector 5.

"Here's our street, Domnul Mike."

"I know."

The telephone clatters into its cradle and Greybeard spreads his arms, gripping the counter. His body language says, *Stay away,* but he says, "How can I help?"

Tina explains, Madeleine explains, then Greybeard explains.

"What the hell. The dog you want is probably dead by now. *Three weeks,* you say? Why didn't you come sooner?" He scratches his beard. It's hard work dealing with idiots. Or perhaps he's got fleas.

"Could you at least check if Linda's still here?" says Tina. "She's nice-looking. Black and brown. Sort of a Rottweiler."

"*Sort of a Rottweiler?* It doesn't matter what sort. Two weeks and we zap 'em. That's the rule. You should've come sooner."

Angela steps forward. "Excuse me, sir, but these ladies didn't try sooner because they can't adopt a dog like Linda. Because they live in small flats and adopted several dogs already. However, my husband and I can adopt a dog. We arrived in Romania two days ago and came here as soon as we could. We're simply asking you to check if Linda is still alive, that's all."

Greybeard seems surprised. "I see. Where did you come from?"

"Azerbaijan."

"So, why didn't you adopt a dog there?"

"Please, sir."

He sighs. "Very well, walk this way. And only you. Not this lot."

"Better if you take Tina or Madeleine. They know the dog."

"Suit yourself, but I haven't got all day."

Madeleine nudges Tina – *you go* – and Tina follows Greybeard.

They return ten minutes later. Tina looks fed up. Madeleine grabs her by the arm.

"Did you find Linda?"

"Not sure. There's one dog that looks like her. Sitting alone. Scared and skinny. I can't tell. I called her name, but–"

Madeleine turns to Greybeard. "May I check, too?"

He gawps at Angela. "Jesus, how long is this going to take?"

"Sir, please let Madeleine try?"

"What, you couldn't find any stray dogs in Afghanistan?"

"We're only trying to help." Tina blows her nose into a hanky.

Greybeard looks ready to blow a fuse. "Yes, of course you are."

He marches out, beckoning Madeleine. I look again at the coloured map on the wall. It represents a modern solution to an old problem, and makes me wonder. *What if Ceaușescu had not forced his citizens to live in tiny apartments, during Romania's so-called Golden Era?* They wouldn't have abandoned their dogs, is what. But he did, and they did, and now look. A map of Bucharest, bright as a rainbow. But it doesn't end in a pot of gold. It ends here, in a concrete yard enclosed by a fence, then with a needle in the arse.

Greybeard returns soon enough, with Madeleine. She can barely speak for weeping. She hugs Tina. "Yes, it's Linda, she's alive!"

"Great, so we can adopt her," says Angela.

"No," says Greybeard, "someone already did, two days ago."

"Pardon?"

"Like I said, that big black one is already adopted." Greybeard walks to a little window in the wall behind him. He slides it back and murmurs to a younger, elfin-faced fellow in the office beyond. The elf smiles at us through the glass. He has short, sticky-up hair, shirt and tie, and an agreeable air. One of life's optimists, I reckon, for whom the stray dog pound is always half-empty. Greybeard returns to the counter and gives a little cough, shuffling papers. He seems to have forgotten all about us.

"If Linda has been adopted," says Angela, "why is she still here?"

Greybeard doesn't even look up. "Why are you still here?"

"We won't leave until you answer the question," I say.

"Very well. The dog is here because the people who adopted it are coming back."

"When?"

"One of these days."

"Perhaps they changed their mind. Could you phone them?"

"No time for that."

"What about your young colleague, next door?"

"Costel is busy, no time."

"We've got time. Could you give us their number, please?"

"Confidential." Greybeard flicks documents, busy being busy. "Come tomorrow and see if that dog is still here. Good day."

Angela plants her elbows on his counter. "It takes us an hour to get here. It would take two minutes to phone those people."

"Sorry, I can't help you."

Madeleine is sobbing quietly into a fist, but that won't help either. Tina caresses her shoulder. "Wasting our time, Maddy."

We troop out, single file, in silence. We're halfway across the car park when a voice calls out, somewhere behind us. "Doamna, stop!"

We stop. Young Costel with the sticky-up hair scoots across glistening tarmac and says to Angela, "You want to see Linda?"

"What's the point? She's been adopted. Apparently."

"Even so, you want to see her? Domnul, how about you?"

"That's why we came, but what difference will it make?"

"Just come, follow me!"

We glance at Tina and Madeleine – *whatever* – and follow Costel towards the yard, where dogs of all shapes and sizes are emerging from cages to yawn, stretch, and lap at puddles. Some bark at us and trot up and down, behind the wire fence. They seem excited rather than aggressive. Madeleine cups a hand to her mouth.

"Linda!"

A large, skinny dog looks up. Madeleine shouts again. The dog bounds forward and stands on hind legs at the fence, whining. Tina reaches through to ruffle brown ears. "Linda, my beauty!"

Linda might have been a beauty once, but no longer. Her ribs and vertebrae are visible and her black coat is patchy. Yes, she's good-looking, keen-eyed, friendly, and seems intelligent, but she's not for us. Even if we could adopt this fierce-looking wretch, she'd freeze in the first Transylvanian winter. Linda is a city dog and already adopted. *So why are we playing lovey-dovey through a fence?* Costel nudges my arm. "This is Linda, isn't it, Domnul?"

"Seems so."

He nudges me again. "And you like her, yes?"

"I'm just glad she'll have a home. Got any fluffy sheepdogs?"

He gives me a wolfish grin. "No, they live in the mountains."

"Never mind. Thanks anyway. Bye Linda. Let's go, Angela."

We walk away, grim-faced, but Costel scurries after us, tugging at Angela's arm. *"Doamna, hai să facem să fie bine."*

Let's find a way, madam.

Angela turns, curious. "What did you say?"

Costel shrugs. "Let's make it ok for everyone. Follow me, please?"

He leads us back to the offices, but this time we enter through a rear door and stand in a corridor. Framed photos of happy dogs line the walls. Costel is smiling. We smile too, but I have no idea why. Perhaps he thinks we're telepathic. Luckily for him, Angela is.

"What, you want a bribe?" she says.

"As I said, let's find a way if you want to adopt Linda."

"Who's already been adopted," I suggest.

"Domnul, let's make everyone happy, including Linda."

"I thought dog adoptions in Romania are free?" says Angela.

"Yes, but let's try if you like."

"Incredible." Angela looks at me. "Well, Mike?"

"I'd say *yes*. She's quite a dog, but she'll freeze in mountains."

"She won't freeze, trust me," says our spiky-haired fixer.

Angela opens her purse. "Here's fifty lei, how's that?"

Costel raises his pixie chin and peeps into her purse.

"What, not enough?" I say, almost laughing. He just smiles.

Angela hands over another fifty. Costel slips the banknotes into a pocket. "This way, please."

Greybeard is busy with a foolscap folder, probably stuffed with money from fools like us. As we enter the reception area for the second time, he looks at Angela, then at his young colleague. His expression gives nothing away; here they give dogs away.

"You're back, Madam." It's not a question, more of a grunt.

"Yes, Linda is available after all. So, do I fill in a form?"

"No, as I said, come tomorrow for an update."

"An *update?* I just gave this guy a hundred lei. So, give me the dog."

Greybeard pulls a face. He seems baffled. "I don't follow."

"Oh, really?" says Angela, "what, you think we're stupid?"

"Stupid?" He pulls another face. From his repertoire.

Now it's my turn. "Give us the dog or give us our money."

"Domnul, adoptions are free."

"I want to speak to your supervisor," says Angela.

"Madam, fill in a complaint form and I'll look into it."

"You'll put it in your bin as soon as we leave."

"Madam, this is not Afghanistan, this is Romania."

"Where dog adoptions are free. Give me the money."

"What money?"

"And your names. For when I call my friends at Pro TV."

"Pro TV?"

Dogs bark in the distance. Our spiky-haired fixer coughs, and slinks away through a door.

Tina tugs Angela's arm. "Doamna Angela, Costel just gave me your money back."

"Creeps," says Madeleine, wiping her nose, "let's go."

"I'm very sorry," says Greybeard, "for any misunderstanding. Call us tomorrow, first thing. If you wish to adopt, bring a work contract and proof of residence. These are the rules. We have to be careful. There are some unscrupulous people out there."

"Not to mention in here," says Angela, and Madeleine laughs.

Trooping across the car park, we see no unscrupulous people. Just dogs locked in a compound.

"I'm done with this place," says Angela, "it's ridiculous."

"But, Doamna, what about poor Linda?" says Tina.

"We'll look for a poor sheepdog," I say, "in our village in Transylvania."

"Hmm, but when will you go, Domnul Mike?"

"By the end of this week we'll be there, *insha'Allah.*"

Tina looks confused. "I never heard of that place."

Our four cats from Azerbaijan couldn't care less about Linda or any other dog, I can tell. They curl on our balcony, snoozing in the midday sun. No rain today, lucky us. Traffic drones along the street below. Bucharest sounds just like Baku, but Transylvania will be different. Green and quiet. With a big, fluffy sheepdog. *Should I warn these lazy cats?* Nah, Angela can tell them when she gets off the phone. I wonder who called.

Angela joins me on the balcony. "That was Tina."

"And?"

"She's got the dog, she's got Linda."

"What?"

"She went back to the pound, this morning, with what's-her-name."

"Madeleine's going to adopt Linda?"

"No, *we* are. Madeleine filed the paperwork. Linda is at a clinic, she's washed and vaccinated. They gave her some vitamin shots. All we have to do is collect her. It's walking distance. Someone at the clinic will transfer ownership to us. To me, actually."

"You agreed to adopt Linda?"

"Why not?"

"You saw Linda's fur, she'll freeze."

"Linda will be fine in a kennel, no problem."

"Says who?"

"The vet at the clinic. Tina asked him. She's very helpful."

"She's a busybody. Linda hates cats. You'll regret this, I bet."

"We'll see. Oh, and we owe Tina fifty lei, don't let me forget."

"She had to pay for the clinic?"

"No, she had to pay those creeps at the dog pound."

"Where adoptions are free? What a scam."

"Look on the bright side, Linda's free."

"You can tell the cats. And mention the big garden."

"I will. Transylvania, here we come."

Red in Tooth and Claw

Radu has a farmer's tan, a lazy smile, and forearms that could throw me over his fence. He stands in his courtyard, sharpening a knife with a six-inch blade that glints in the morning sun. He thanks me for coming. I ask him how he feels about killing animals. He shrugs, glancing at distant mountains shrouded in pale grey mist.

"Did my first pig when I was ten. Difficult, that was, but not anymore. Come, you can help."

He walks to a gloomy shed and murmurs to a beautiful brown calf inside it. He nudges the timid animal into the sunny yard, wrestles it to the ground, trusses its hind legs together, and opens its neck with his blade. He rises without a word, and stands back. Job done.

The calf makes no sound. Blood flows and hooves kick. An inquisitive white cat prowls nearby; it sees what we're up to and probably knows that this brief carnage means a long feast, sooner or later. The calf stares at the cat with eyes that acquire a milky glaze as the minutes pass. I'm wondering what to say to Radu. His calm expertise is impressive, if that's the right word, but questions remain.

"Radu, why didn't you stun the calf?"

"Stun it? Too painful. Put it this way, how would you like a whack in the head with a hammer? Plus, a stun gun is too expensive. Anyway, time to skin this in the barn. Grab a leg."

We drag the dead calf across the grass, leaving a slimy, scarlet trail. Radu slings the rope around a crossbeam and we hoist the calf upside down, until it dangles a few inches above the ground. He pulls a Swiss Army penknife from his pocket and makes careful incisions in the carcass. *Cut and tug, cut and tug.* The hide gapes and drapes, freshly peeled. The farm cat approaches and crouches below the carcass, lapping at a pool of dark blood; its white head is soon spattered with red, as if painted by Jackson Pollock. *Vampire Puss.*

Radu is hacking gently at the hide. *Cut and tug, cut and tug.* It's tough work and he's breathing hard. "You like a bit of tasty veal, eh, Mike?" He has a mischievous twinkle in his eye, as so often. "Oh, sorry, I forgot. Vegetarian, right?"

"Right, Radu."

"Since when?"

"1982."

"1982? I wasn't even born." He stands back, pointing his blade at the carcass. "I need a rest. Want to try?"

"OK."

"Don't puncture the hide."

"What happens if I do?"

"I'll string you up by your ankles, is what." Radu gives me a gap-toothed smile, and his bloody penknife.

The carcass sways gently on its rope, like a punch bag. The sight of the bloodied beast reminds me of that line by Tennyson: *Nature, red in tooth and claw.* Oh well, here goes.

The exposed flesh is greyish pink and warm to the touch. Holding the knife in my right hand, I cut the skin, and tug at the hide with my left, wondering what I'm doing here. Radu folds his arms and watches me, as if wondering the same.

The answer is that we all need help sometimes, and today is my turn to help him, if that's what I'm doing. Because he's one of our neighbours and I owe him a favour or three. His bubbly wife Raluca often brings us eggs and cheese. That's how it is up here – they've been kind to us since we moved to the village a few months ago, and now we're friends, close to the land. Or trying to be, in my case, which is why I'm puzzled that Radu asked me to help slaughter a calf. Perhaps he's testing the newcomer with this *rite de passage*.

I lean closer, working the blade from left to right, across and down. *Don't puncture the hide.* It's hard to believe that this creature was alive and well, just a short while ago. What a way to die, poor thing. Then again, a flashing knife to the jugular vein is perhaps more humane and less stressful than a bumpy ride to some clanking abattoir reeking of stale blood. And Radu's probably right about that hammer. *No thanks.*

I do my best, but stand back after ten minutes to let Radu take over. He works quickly, removing the rest of the hide, then uses a bigger knife for butchering the carcass.

His impromptu biology lesson is grimly illuminating. I learn the location and function of the various internal organs, and how his wife will cook them. He shoves his forearm deep into the guts, extracts a translucent pouch and cuts it open to reveal a chalky deposit.

"We add this white stuff to our cheese."

I peep at the white stuff in the pouch. It's rennet, probably. It's certainly time for me to leave because this musty barn seems warmer by the minute and smells sickly sweet. The dead calf's head is in a bucket of crimson water and mine is in need of fresh air.

Stretch your Mind

"You want to offer a yoga class? Here in our village?" Doamna Miruna seems concerned. Worry lines kink her smooth brow as she considers Angela's suggestion. We're hoping Miruna might prove a helpful ally, well-connected woman that she is, but something is wrong.

She stares at us, shading her eyes from the fierce sun. It warms the church steps beneath our feet, but the atmosphere has turned rather chilly. Our local VIP looks increasingly ill at ease, as Angela elaborates.

"Yes, Miruna, yoga. I plan to offer an introductory class and invite local women. They've probably never had the chance to do yoga, and might enjoy it. You can come too, if you like."

Miruna places a hand on her chest, as though honoured – or scandalised – by the invitation. "Me?"

"Why not?" says Angela. "My first class will be free. I'll only charge if people want more sessions, just to cover rent of the hall. It's an ideal venue. I could put posters in the windows, what do you think?"

Miruna seems preoccupied. Stressed, even. "Sorry, posters in whose windows?"

"The windows in the Cultural Centre."

Angela points towards a medium-sized, one-storey, white-walled building, nearby. The sign above the entrance says *Căminul Cultural,* but that fat brass padlock on the door seems to have other ideas, which is probably why nothing ever happens in that place except, apparently, an annual dance and traditional fisticuffs at New Year. Nevertheless, we'll try. This is why we've stopped by the church, after all. Miruna is a hard lady to track down, but this is where one can find her, about now, every Sunday. How convenient that we were passing.

Miruna folds her arms, thinking it over. She's very slim. Perfect for yoga. Long in the torso; probably suffers from lower back trouble, as do I. Yoga would help. She looks at me and winces.

"Yoga, Domnul Mike?"

"Yes, Doamna Miruna, but the thing is, we're not sure who to ask about offering a class here. So, we thought we'd ask you, seeing as your husband is a local councillor. Any idea how Angela might rent the hall? Given your contacts, we were hoping that –"

Miruna raises her palm, cutting me off in my conjunction. "Yoga is from India, I believe. Hindu, isn't it, Doamna Angela?"

"I believe so, yes."

"That's why we don't need it in our village. We have the church, you see." Miruna turns and gestures towards it, with a beatific gaze. God is behind her. We are below. The big bell bongs above. I won't ask for whom, because I already know.

"But yoga is not about religion," says Angela, "it's just gentle stretching, deep breathing, and finding yourself through meditation."

"We can find ourselves through prayer." Miruna offers a winning smile. You lose.

Driving home, past fragrant meadows where wildflowers bloom and moo-cows moo, my wife doesn't say much. Too disappointed, probably. She needs cheering up.

"Angela, I have an idea. Let's build a Hindu temple in our garden. Buy lots of monkeys from India. Invite some Hare Krishna devotees to have a procession round the village. Get-it-on, bang-a-gong."

She smiles, eventually. "Be serious."

"OK. Why not offer a class on our terrace?"

"That's a better idea."

"And never mind Miruna. It's not her village. People here might like yoga. At least, they deserve a chance to try it."

"You know why she's worried?"

"No idea."

"Because of Bivolaru."

"Water buffaloes?"

"No, that's *bivoli*. Bivolaru taught yoga in Romania during the communist era. They put him in prison, even a psychiatric hospital, I think. Charged him with all sorts. Yoga was banned. Even now, as soon as you mention *yoga* to most Romanians, all they can think of is Bivolaru, in other words, the bad guy. Yoga means Bivolaru. Perhaps that's another reason Miruna is wary."

"Except she didn't mention him."

"On the steps of the church? She'd be scared in case she goes to hell."

"That's her problem. We're going to teach yoga. Well, you are."

"But if I put posters up, someone will tear them down."

"Fair point. Why don't you just phone or text anyone who might be interested?"

"Could work. I'll ask them in person, too. Tell the ladies all about breathing, relaxing, stretching, curing aches and pains, solving back problems, finding yourself in meditation."

"Let's hope the ladies don't tell Miruna, or you'll find yourself on the rack."

Kissed by the Blade

Difficult, this scything lark. The land slopes at a steep angle, making balance tricky as you swing right to left. The tough grass is dry and resilient, so you have to sharpen your blade every few minutes if you know how. I don't. I run my whetstone along the curved steel, hoping for the best. Sounds like fingernails scraping on a blackboard. We never studied scything in school.

"Not like that, Domnul Mike." Our neighbour Vlad chuckles at me through the gaps in our fence. He's in the dirt road beyond, a scythe slung across his broad shoulders, and grinning like a Transylvanian cat. He beckons me towards him. "Give it here."

I offer my scythe. He squints down the blade, turns it this way and that, handling the fearsome tool with the dexterity of one who knows, as opposed to one who hasn't got a clue. As so often in Vlad's presence, I feel pretty useless. But, looking on the bright side, his intervention provides a welcome break. Sweat trickles down my aching back. It's about 30°C, out here, according to the top of my head. According to Shakespeare, *Sometime too hot the eye of heaven shines.* Bang on, Bard.

"Needs a beating." says Vlad.

"A beating?"

Vlad thrusts the scythe at me. "This does, your *coasă*."

"How do you mean?"

Vlad sighs. "God help us. What you doing tomorrow?"

I point at the overgrown yard. "Cutting this lot, or trying."

He shakes his head. "First, learn how. I'll show you, if you like. Six o'clock, tomorrow. Be ready. Bring your *coasă*." Vlad gestures towards the high slopes beyond the village. "We'll go up to my land. You got football boots?"

"No, why?"

"Never mind. Anyway, do you want to learn how to cut grass?"

"Sure, but when you say *six*, do you mean in the morning?"

He looks at me as if I'm soft in the head, as well as blunt in the blade. "Yes, 6 a.m. We start early and finish late. Up to you."

He strides off, whistling a sweet tune and rocking his scythe. *6 a.m.?* I'll need an early night for my day with The Happy Reaper.

Next morning, six sharp, no Vlad. I sit on our bench, waiting. And waiting. Perhaps he's forgotten, but I just remembered something: if there's one thing about Vlad that you can rely on, it's that he's unreliable. He means well, always helpful, but tends to promise more than he delivers. *Didn't we wait five weeks for him to drill three holes in our wall?* He let us down with the roof tiles, too, as I recall. And yesterday, he said *6 a.m.* That was almost an hour and a half ago. He's a bugger and I'm bored. *Fetch guitar.*

I go into the house, grab a guitar, and return to wait on the bench, wondering what to play. Ah, yes: *I Should Have Known Better.* Trust them Beatles, love 'em or loath 'em, a song for every occasion. I wonder if Vlad has a watch? Oh well, *strum strum.*

I watch the lane and tap my toe. For my next song, I'd like to play *If 6 Was 9,* by Jimi Hendrix. Or perhaps I'll eat my sandwiches. They're in my knapsack. Maybe I'll just eat one, seeing as I haven't had breakfast. Because I was in a bit of a rush. To be ready so early. *Hmm, a cheese sandwich at half-seven in the morning?* Bit early for lunch. Perhaps I'll write a song entitled *Where The Hell Is Vlad?* All you need is three chords, as they say. And ninety minutes. I glance at my watch. Ninety-five, actually.

"Perhaps he forgot?" The voice comes from above, like that of an angel dispensing wisdom. I look up. My wife is looking down from the open window of our bedroom. Her chin is cupped in her palms. She yawns, pointing at grey mountains smouldering in the sun. "Nice day, at least. Phone him, Mike."

"I prefer to play my guitar, it's a nice day, why not?"

"You could cut our grass."

"I'd love to, but Vlad said I need lessons."

"Vlad says lots of things. I have a better idea – why don't we just *pay* someone to cut our grass? You should stick to writing books."

"If we're going to live in these mountains, I might as well learn how. Besides, it's good exercise."

"Up to you. Where are our dogs? Should be awake by now."

"Still in bed, like sensible people. You ready for coffee?"

"Love some. Shall I come down or will you bring it up?"

She smiles sweetly and we both know the answer. I place my guitar next to my knapsack. My scythe seems safe enough, resting by the wall. *Where's my whetstone?* Ah, yes, in this plastic holder on my belt. Such items are essential when you go grass cutting. If you ever do. I glance down the empty lane. *Yeah, right.*

Angela sits up in bed, propped on her pillows, sipping coffee.

"Nice, thanks, Mike."

She peers over the rim of the New York mug. It's the one we bought during our honeymoon in 1997, showing the Twin Towers. They don't make mugs like that anymore. Probably a collector's item now, for all the wrong reasons. I stand at the bedroom window, watching the lane. No Vlad.

"It's almost 8 a.m., you should call him," says Angela.

"Talk of the devil, here he comes, around the corner. Most of his family, too, by the look of it. I'd better go, mustn't keep them waiting, after all. Bye, mwah!"

I blow a kiss across the room and scamper downstairs.

Out in the yard, I find my knapsack upside down on the grass. Silver foil flutters in the breeze. Our dogs are munching my sandwiches and wagging their tails in appreciation. *Tasty, thanks.*

It's going to be one of those days.

The narrow dirt lane to Vlad's land is long and winding. He walks in the middle, whistling God knows what. His wife Bella and teenaged daughter Cătălina walk on either side of him. They're each carrying a scythe. I walk behind, carrying mine. They're all wearing shorts, T-shirts, and floppy sun hats. They've got strong legs from years of tramping these unforgiving hills. It's a hard life for mountain folk. *Hmm, how come they're all wearing football boots, too, even the ladies? Happy Reapers FC?*

Bella turns and says, "How's Doamna Angela, Mike?"

"She's well, thanks Bella, having a lie-in."

Vlad chuckles. "At this hour, Mike?"

"She worked late, last night. You got a watch, Vlad?"

"Never wear one. No need. Why?"

"Because you said *six.*"

"Six what?"

"Six o'clock. I was up at five-thirty."

"So was I."

"Our cow had a calf," says Bella, by way of explanation.

"And don't forget," says Vlad, "I need to beat your scythe, Mike, so make sure you remind me." He resumes whistling.

Cătălina drops back and we walk side by side. I ask her about school, as you do, and she says, "Summer holidays, now."

"Right. By the way, do you still want to be a policewoman?"

"Who, me?"

"You said you wanted to be a cop. That time I gave you a lift."

"Not anymore."

"Right. Any idea what you'll do when you leave school?"

"Get a job. A normal one. There's a factory in Brașov."

Her phone rings and that's that. Vlad turns around and gives me a wink. "Sorry I was late, Domnul Mike, our cow needed help."

"Fair enough. So, how's the calf doing?"

"Real beauty, all black," says Bella, tugging at a black bra strap. Her black singlet has black sequins; it matches her dyed black hair and baggy black shorts. Black mascara rings her tired eyes. She looks like Alice Cooper. Except for the shorts, maybe. Cătălina is giggling into her phone. Vlad is whistling. I'm wondering about those football boots. Who cares. *School's Out*, as Alice said.

"Bear!" Vlad drops to one knee, a few metres ahead of me, in the middle of the potholed lane. Bella and Cătălina squat alongside him. I stop dead and sink into a crouch, my heart racing.

"You're right," says Bella, quietly.

"Well-spotted," says Cătălina.

I'm looking into the trees alongside us. Down the lane. Across the valley. *Where's the bloody bear? Which way do we run?*

"Mike, what are you doing?" Vlad is looking back at me.

"You said *bear*."

"I meant this." He chuckles, beckoning me. Keeping low, I crab forwards. Vlad points to the ground. I look down and see a paw print in the dust. It's perfect, as big as a plate, with an oval depression in the centre, indentations from five toes, and some claw marks. Vlad points up the lane at several identical prints.

"Recent, too. But cars will erase them, by noon."

When we reach the family plot, Bella indicates the boundaries.

"We'll start here, Domnul Mike, and work down to the fence at the bottom of the hill. Watch how we do it, first, then join us."

Their land is about the size of a football field, on a steep slope dotted with birch trees. My three companions assemble side by side, in a loose row. Vlad is in the middle. They swing their scythes in wide arcs as they advance, step by step, shaving the slope and each leaving a neat trail of cut grass and wildflowers. Their blades make a gentle swishing sound. I walk behind, watching closely. "You folks are good. Faster than me."

Vlad pauses to wipe his brow. "Easy when you know, Mike."

"How do you manage to cut the grass so short?"

"Blade must be sharp and straight. You twist like this, watch."

Vlad plants his legs wide apart and bent slightly at the knees, then rotates his upper body, right to left, right to left, swinging his scythe down and across. The fresh cut grass flops sideways. Easy.

"Football boots for grip, Mike."

"Now I get it. And here was me thinking–"

"Anyway, enough yap. I'll beat your *coasă*, then it's your turn."

Vlad lays down his scythe, rummages in a canvas bag, and takes out a wooden plug the size of an avocado pear, worn smooth with use. One end has a shiny tip made of lead.

"What's that?" I ask.

"Nicovala." Vlad takes a hammer and whacks the *nicovala* into the ground until only the lead tip is visible. "Your *coasă*, Mike?"

I pass him my scythe. He takes it in one hand and lies down, on his side, next to the *nicovala*. Propped on his elbow, he cradles the scythe's wooden shaft in the crook of his arm, so the blade rests on the lead tip of the *nicovala*. He taps with his hammer along the blade. *Tap-tap, tap-tap.* He pauses to point at the blade.

"Beating flattens any kinks along the edge, see?"

I lean in, for a closer look, none the wiser. "Right."

Vlad taps away for a few minutes then flips the scythe over and beats the other side of the blade. "Done, now let's sharpen her."

He stands up, sets the blade against his knee, and runs his whetstone back and forth, fast and hard, along both sides of the blade. It looks a bit risky. You could lose the top of your finger.

"Ever get hurt doing this, Vlad?"

"Yes, in the early days. *Kissed by the blade,* as we say."

For a final flourish, Vlad seizes a handful of freshly-cut grass and wipes the glinting edge, up and down. He tosses the grass aside and spins my scythe vertically on its shaft, grinning at me.

"She's all ready for you, Domnul Mike."

"*Mulțumesc.*"

"*Cu plăcere.* Let's see how you do. Try on this bit, here."

I plant my legs apart, angle the scythe at a patch of grass, twist my hips to the right and swing to the left. *Swooosh.* The blade cuts like a razor, but I'm no barber. Vlad clicks his teeth and shakes his head. "Try for a wider arc, like Cătălina."

I shade my eyes and watch his daughter. Her blade slices gracefully through the wildflowers as she moves slowly downhill. She's wearing earphones and bobbing her head. Swathes of grass flutter in her wake and Vlad shoots me a wink. *That's my girl.*

Mid-morning, we pause, hot and panting, to sit cross-legged under a shady tree. Bella opens a rucksack of food, teases me about how my dogs ate my sandwiches, and invites me to grab some hard-boiled eggs, salami, chunks of cheese, rough bread, whatever I like – it's all here. She takes a nip of hooch and Vlad swigs on a beer. Cătălina wanders off, chatting to her phone. The sun glitters through the foliage. My forearms ache from an hour and a half of relentless twist-and-hack, twist-and-hack. My lower back is numb. *And it's what, only 11 a.m.?* I can hardly see my watch because stinging sweat dribbles into my eyes.

Vlad munches bread. "How you feelin', Domnul Mike?"

"Knackered, but my scythe cuts better than before."

"Sharp blade, see. I'll beat it again when we get back."

When we get back, it's 9 p.m. and I'm in a zombie trance. Even rooting my key from a pocket seems an effort, since my arms feel rubbery and longer than they were twelve hours ago. That's when I was a bit annoyed with my tardy neighbours, but since then, I've seen how hard they work. All summer long? *Respect* is the word.

We say goodbye and Bella thanks me for my efforts. Cătălina wiggles a hand in my general direction and walks on, yapping into her phone, *No way, says who?* Vlad asks how much he owes me for my help. I shake my tired head.

"No way, I learned a lot today, we're square."

We slap high-fives. Even that hurts. As they amble home down the lane, Vlad turns to ask, "Same time, tomorrow, Mike?"

I point at our overgrown yard. "Tomorrow, I cut this lot."

"Spor la treabă," says Bella. *Good luck with that.*

Sleep comes quickly and I rise early next day, keen to get *swooshing* in nice wide arcs before the sun reaches its zenith. I emerge from the house, ready for work. Our dogs circle me with waggy tails and bright eyes. *Where's your knapsack?*

By 8.30 a.m., I've sliced my way through 100 square metres of thick grass, wildflowers, and tenacious weeds. Not bad, but I've got another 1,900 square metres to go. Quite a big yard, this, especially when you're knee deep in resilient, alpine vegetation. My scythe has a few visible kinks but I'm keeping it sharp. Whetstone every five minutes. *Probably time to do it again.*

I stand with one leg bent and rest the blade against my knee, just like Vlad. I scrape the whetstone along the inside edge of the dull steel, back and forth, up and down, hard and fast, until it glints. I change position, spin the scythe vertically on its shaft, and sharpen the other side, watching sparks fly. When both sides of the blade are done, I pause and look at the mountains, enjoying the cool air of early morning and the spectacular views. *How I love this peace and quiet.* Better than some big, mucky city, any day.

For my final flourish, I grab a handful of freshly-cut grass and wipe it quickly down the metre-long blade. A sharp, blinding pain shoots up my arm and kicks me in the head.

Mother of God.

I drop the scythe and the grass. Blood weeps into my palm. From a gaping wound three centimetres long, across the pad of my thumb.

Fuck, what have I done?

I seize it with my good hand, press hard, and raise my arm to reduce circulation. I walk quickly towards the house, whimpering in shock. Blood trickles down my forearm and pools in the crook of my elbow. *Kissed by the blade?* Damn right. Love hurts.

I trot up steps, woozy-headed. I'll need a dressing, a bandage, and adhesive surgical tape. I'll ask Angela to help. She was right, as so often. *We should pay someone to cut our grass.* And I should stick to writing, while I've still got my bloody fingers.

Dog Willing

The stout women are ten metres ahead of me and trudging three abreast up the long, narrow lane to our mountain village, shaded from the fierce midsummer sun by an arching canopy of foliage. I toot the car's horn to let them know I'm coming, but they don't seem to notice. Too busy chatting.

Each woman wears a brightly-coloured headscarf, big gold hoop earrings, a baggy blouse, and a lurid, flowing skirt. I reckon they're Roma, although we rarely see such folks and none live up here. Their big wicker baskets – two apiece – are filled with something brownish white – mushrooms, probably. Perhaps the women hope to sell them to locals.

Hearing my car approach, they turn their heads quickly to look downhill, then drop their baskets and wave: *Domnul, give us a lift!* Their podgy, middle-aged faces glisten with sweat. They're too old for this work, worn out, desperate even.

Alone in the car, I apply my brakes, buying time to think. *Should I offer them a ride up this murderous slope?* Common decency says *yes,* especially since no public transport reaches our village, and they all look seriously overweight on Heart Attack Hill in hot weather.

But common sense says *no,* because I have painful memories of the day, many years ago, when a burly Roma scam artist floored me with a lightning-fast, jaw-crunching wallop. On the other hand, he was a professional Bucharest scallywag, whereas these women have been working hard in the woods, by the look of it. *What are they going to do, whack me with a mushroom and steal my car?*

I stop, flash my headlights, and they all hurry downhill, wobbling and grinning. They clamber aboard. I ask them to wear seat belts but they shake their heads and the woman in the passenger seat says, "No need for that, Mister."

So I ask again, explaining that if they don't buckle up, they'll have to walk. Their pearly smiles freeze and their dark eyes glitter. *No need for that, Mister.* The woman alongside me fastens her belt and the two in the back follow suit, tugging and tutting. Within moments, they're all trussed up like good little girls.

"This music, Domnul, what is it?" says the one sitting alongside me.

"Louis Armstrong, do you like it?"

"Not much. Have you got any good music?"

I stop the CD. "Let's just chat. Are you coming to Culmea?"

"No, Domnul, we're going to Dâmbu Vechi."

"Dâmbu Vechi? That's a long walk, ladies."

"Thank you, we'd be very grateful."

"Actually, ladies, I didn't mean–"

"God will smile on you today, Domnul."

"And for the rest of your life, Domnul."

"What a nice car you have, Domnul."

"Are you married, dearest Domnul?"

"Of course he is, sister, don't you see the wedding ring?"

"Ah yes, the ring."

"Your wife is a lucky woman, Domnul."

"And so are we, sisters, since he took pity on us."

"God be praised."

I glance in my rear-view mirror. The two jolly chatterboxes on the back seat are blessing themselves – once, twice, thrice. The one in the passenger seat is staring at my wedding ring. Me, I'm in the driving seat, or at least I was.

Dâmbu Vechi? The only road that leads down there is long and treacherous. I'll need to make another decision: *Goodbye or another good turn?*

I drive slowly uphill, mulling my options. If I go straight home, I'll first have to drop off my three exhausted passengers about twenty seconds from now, on the brow of this hill, at the left turn for Dâmbu Vechi. I won't feel good when I break the bad news and ask them to get out of this comfy, air-conditioned car and nor will they, facing a five-mile walk under that blazing sun. I can just imagine their reaction: *Big help that was, Mister, careful you don't turn into a frog.* On the other hand, the road down to Dâmbu Vechi gets hellish steep and very narrow in places, especially for a car this big. Meet a vehicle coming the other way and you're in a fix; it means reversing two hundred metres to the previous passing place. Isn't that why my wife and I swore never to use that road again if we can possibly avoid it? Yes, exactly. *So what do I do?*

The woman in the passenger seat is yapping about how they'll get a bus from Dâmbu Vechi to Brașov and arrive home before dark. "Just in time to feed the kids. I've got ten, Domnul."

"Really? That's a lot of work, you must get tired."

"Yes, up since 4 a.m. That's how you find the best mushrooms, but I won't say where. You might pick 'em, then what will I sell in the market?"

She's friendly and fun. The sort of person, in fact, that you feel you've known all your life. I realise why: she looks a bit like my mum, with a ready smile and the same irrepressible, can-do spirit. Churchill in a skirt, digging for victory, doing her best against difficult odds. As opposed to a selfish man in a big car. That'll be me. It's probably a sign. There's another one coming up, on our left, nailed to a tree.

She points a finger. "What does that say? I don't read so well."

"Dâmbu Vechi."

"In that case, you have to turn left soon, Domnul."

"Because that's where we want to go, Domnul."

"Sign says Dâmbu Vechi, Domnul."

"Yes, ladies, I know. I made it."

"You made that sign, Domnul?"

"Yes, last summer, to help tourists who get lost."

"Are you a tourist who got lost, Domnul?"

"Sort of, I suppose. Actually, I live here."

"You *live* here? Well, I never. And does your dear wife like Romania?"

"She's Romanian."

"You married a Romanian?" She stares at me, then turns to her colleagues on the rear seat. "He married a Romanian."

"We're not deaf. Ask him if she's pretty, go on."

The woman upfront turns back. "Is she pretty, Domnul?"

"Very. She's from Muntenia. Lots of pretty girls there."

"We've never been. Have we been there, sister?"

"No, sister. Ask him if he has any kids."

"Do you have kids, Domnul?"

"No."

"Maybe God will grant you some, in time."

"Here's our left turn for Dâmbu Vechi, tell him."

"Mister, here's the turn, like your helpful sign said."

"You should make some more signs, Domnul."

"Turn, Domnul. Turn now or you'll miss it."

The car lurches left. They've put a spell on me, these friendly gypsy women. What the hell, I'll go along for the ride. They seem nice enough and I'm in no hurry, after all. The car smells of mushrooms and honest toil. They're not violent scallywags like that guy in Bucharest. Perhaps I'll take them halfway to Dâmbu Vechi. Or maybe three quarters.

When we arrive in Dâmbu Vechi, bumping around the last of the steep bends, they ask me where the bus stop is.

"Because we don't know and it might be a long walk," says the woman alongside me, fluttering her eyelashes. It's a clever line, and, as my mum would say, *She's all there with her onions*. Or here, I suppose, with all her mushrooms.

I drive towards the centre of the sleepy little town. "I'll drop you at the main road, ок? I've seen buses there."

"Domnul, we are completely in your hands, after all."

"And whatever happens, God will shine his light on you."

"This very day, Domnul, as I live and breathe."

"Thank you, ladies, let's hope so, eh?"

A floppy-eared puppy scuttles across the road and I slam my brakes. The women gasp and clutch their baskets. The pup slithers into a culvert. Probably a stray. Won't last long on this road, unless it wises up.

"Well spotted, Domnul, that was close."

"But we need to catch a bus, Domnul, so drive on."

"Domnul, what are you waiting for?"

"To see if the pup runs out again. I don't want to hit it."

Sure enough, the pup re-emerges to circle a dumpster, sniffing for scraps. It's about three months old. Beige back, white chest, and waddling around on oversized paws.

I slide my window down and click my tongue. The pup turns and looks straight at me, head cocked. *Cute or what.* Its pointy muzzle, thick coat, and bushy tail suggest a German Shepherd with a dash of Husky. A broad white stripe runs down the middle of the face, and the ears flop forward at the tips but might straighten up, in time. And such a nose – pink and black, like something you might buy in a joke shop. Nice pup, that, and our dog Linda could use some company; she's Billy No Mates these days and must miss her old social life as a Bucharest stray.

"Domnul, we need to find the bus stop."

"Sorry, ladies, I'm just thinking."

"About that dog? Probably lives around here."

"Maybe not. Looks lost to me. Maybe I'll take it home."

"Domnul, you can't steal someone's dog. What if they see you?"

"*They* who? I reckon that pup has been abandoned."

"How can you tell?"

"Just a hunch. It knows about the culvert and the bin, and is scavenging on the only road into town, which is an ideal place to dump a dog because it will find food, or even get spotted and adopted by someone driving past, like me."

"But that doesn't mean you should."

Now she even sounds like my mum. Her colleagues tut and sigh behind us, equally unconvinced and keen to move on. Maybe they're right. And after all, what do I know of street life in Romania, compared to them?

I drive slowly away but cannot resist a quick glance in the mirror. The pup is staring at the car.

The women weep when I drop them at the bus stop, either because they're so grateful for my help or because they were hoping I'd drive them to Brașov. But seeing as that would be a ninety-minute round trip, it's out of the question, and they're out of my car. Me too, stretching my legs. "Bye, ladies, safe trip home, *drum bun.*"

"*Mulțumesc.*" My former navigator is dabbing her eyes. Her mascara is smudged and she looks like a panda. "Our greetings to your pretty wife."

"Domnul, may your children grow strong and healthy."

"When you have some, we mean."

"Yes, when you have some, and may they live long."

"May the Lord bless you for your kindness."

"God will reward you, this very day."

"And shine his light on your home, forever."

"We cannot thank you enough."

"Our hearts will be full of gratitude. While we wait for a bus."

Their baskets are full of big mushrooms but they don't offer me any. Business is business, perhaps. We shake hands and they wobble off to the bus stop. I slide into the car and cruise away, *toot-toot*. They don't wave. Too busy reading the bus schedule, or trying their best. What a life.

The cute pup is still at the dumpster when I drive by, slowly, on my way home. I park a few metres away, for a little think. *It's what, fifteen minutes since I first spotted this little dog?* Surely long enough for its mother or siblings to have turned up. Street dogs stick together, that much I know. So, either it's wandered out of a local garden or has been abandoned. I'm hoping the latter is true because I want a second dog. A nice-looking dog. *That dog?* Somehow, this feels like destiny and with a flash of celestial insight, I realise: *God will reward you, this very day*. God just did, ladies?

I open the console between the front seats. Sure enough, I'm in luck, because it contains half a pack of oatmeal biscuits. *Do pups like HobNobs?* I exit the car, wait for a gap in traffic, and cross the road. The pup disappears into the culvert but peeps out when I call. Spotting the biscuit in my hand, it wriggles from its hiding place and runs towards me on rubbery legs. *Gimme.* The biscuit is gone in seconds, along with any doubts I might've had. The pup nips my fingers, ravenous, in search of more. Surely, this is a stray. But what beautiful, light brown eyes. They gaze into my soul as only doggy eyes can. I scoop the pup up. It whimpers, licking my hand. I nuzzle its tufty ear and whisper sweet nothings. They seem to work.

Walking back to my car, I notice a man watering his garden. He's noticed me, too. *You can't just steal someone's dog.*

I hoist my prize aloft. "Excuse me, sir, is this your pup?"

He shakes his head and looks at his flowers. "Nope."

"Does it live with one of your neighbours, perhaps?"

He shakes his head. "Been under that bin for a week, that dog."

"Because someone dumped it, perhaps?"

He hoses down a bed of rhododendrons. "Probably."

"What if I take it home?"

"Free country."

"Thanks for your time. Sorry to interrupt. Nice roses."

"Better last year. *Drum bun,* Domnul."

He waves his hose, by way of goodbye; it casts a silver mist of water in the air, like a blessing from a holy man.

Back in the car, the pup cowers in fright when I start the engine. I tickle its ears, *there there.* It rolls belly up and I notice a minor biological detail that I've missed until now.

"You're a girl. Perhaps I'll call you Rose. Or Rhododendron." Then again, there's no rush. We've got all the time in the world. "Want to hear some Louis Armstrong, little girl?"

The beautiful pup is panting at me. Or even smiling, and I have a feeling we'll be good friends from this day on. *Hmm, there's an idea.* Today is Saturday. Perhaps I'll call her *Sam,* short for *Sâmbătă.* Yes, *Sam,* why not? Sounds nice and suits her, sort of. Cute but confident.

Halfway home, my phone rings. The screen says *Angela.* I park under a tree and take the call. My wife tells me that her trip to Bucharest is going ок but her cousin's marriage is falling apart; the husband beats her up. He sounds like a right psychopath and goes to church every Sunday.

"Anyway, Mike, what's new with you? Driving, you say?"

"Yes, up from Dâmbu Vechi."

"From Dâmbu Vechi? On that terrible road?"

"Oops."

"*Oops?* You'll wreck our suspension, Mike. Why did you drive to Dâmbu Vechi? Didn't we agree not to use that road?"

"I picked up three women."

"You picked up three women?"

"They were walking to Dâmbu Vechi, carrying big baskets. I felt sorry for them. They looked all hot and bothered, from picking mushrooms. They were Roma, I think."

"You picked up three women and took a five-mile detour to Dâmbu Vechi, on that terrible road? I can't believe my ears."

"Anyway, it's done. Now I'm driving home."

"Good, take it slowly and please don't offer anyone else a ride, unless they're going to our village."

"I already did. She's going to our village, as you say."

"Fair enough, anyone we know?"

"No, she's new around here. Her name is Sam. Very sweet. Young and rather beautiful. Lovely brown eyes. Gorgeous, actually."

"Really? And when will you drop her off, soon, I hope?"

"I've invited her to stay with me, as you're away."

Some silences might be golden but this one is a bit black. Like the nose of the pup that just puked in our car. Perhaps that's the reward those ladies were talking about.

Bewitched

Two hundred years ago, our neighbours might have called Doamna Dița a witch and burned her alive. Now, they just call her a witch. Well, some do.

Dița lives in a black house with a black cat. She gathers herbs in the forest. She's eighty-six years old, with a wrinkled face and sharp tongue. You get the picture, and Dița gets sarky comments behind her back. Also, she finds the best wild mushrooms and won't say where, because they fetch good prices at local guest houses and she risks life and limb to pick them. She will, however, gift some mushrooms to her friends. In my experience, she's generous to a fault, but even so…

"Watch out, here comes the witch," mutters my middle-aged neighbour Mihai. He leans back against our fence, chuckling, as Dița shuffles up the dirt lane, laden down with two bulging, worn-out canvas bags full of who-knows-what. Mihai nudges my ribs, *It's a joke.* Unless you're the punchline, of course. It's a pity Dița can't turn Mihai into a newt. That, I would laugh at.

Dița stops a few paces from us, wincing as she leans sideways to let her bags slide from her frail shoulders to the ground. She looks tired but, as always, has a certain style. Today, she wears baggy black linen pants, a faded military jacket, and espadrilles. Easily the best-dressed pensioner in our village? Despite her years, she's a strikingly handsome woman – all cheekbones, and deep-set eyes of sapphire blue. Quite a catch in her prime, I bet. Ever the lady, she greets us like the gentlemen we should be.

"Bună ziua, Domnilor."

We reply, in unison. *"Bună ziua, Doamna Dița."*

"So, Domnul Mike, what are you two fellows up to?"

"Just chatting. Mihai was passing by. How about you?"

"Been in the forest." Dița cranes her scrawny neck, checking our house. "Is Doamna Angela home? Brought you some stuff."

"Yes, Angela's home. Care to come in for a cup of tea?"

Dița's smile is a cracker. "Tea would be nice, Domnul Mike."

She reaches for her heavy bags but I carry them for her. As we walk towards the house, I glance back. "Coming in, Mihai?"

He grimaces and slips away. Wary of spells, perhaps.

Dița saunters about, eyeing our kitchen. She pauses to tilt her head at an African mask. *Why would anyone stick that on their wall?* She flops into a chair. Her cracked lips pout as she gazes long and hard at our bookshelf, with steady, owlish interest.

Angela fills our kettle. "How have you been, Doamna Dița?"

"Not so bad, Doamna Angela, you?"

"Fine, thanks, although we could use a little sun."

"Sun will come when it's ready. Want some mushrooms?"

"No thanks, I've read too many scary stories, recently."

"*Pah*. You don't know what you're missing. I got a beauty, look."

Dița coaxes a mushroom from one of her bags, and holds it up. I stare in wonder. *Bloody Nora.* The stem is as broad as a can of Coke and the silken beige top is almost as big as a Dacia hubcap.

"Wow," says Angela.

"Still not interested?" says Dița.

"Sorry, no. Besides, you could make good money on that."

"Don't worry, I will. Hmm, what else have I got in here? Ah, brought you some of this." Dița places a bunch of bright purple flowers on our table. "Wild basil, very good for the heart. Reduces inflammation. Helps depression, too, if you ever get it." Dița plucks a few of the purple flowers, rubs them between her palms, then opens her hands. "Just you smell that, Domnul."

I lean in and inhale the aroma. "Lovely, like Gucci cologne."

Dița gives me a look. "Like *what?*"

"Well, oranges and lemons. It's a long time since I bought any. Gucci cologne, I mean. But, you know how it is, with smells?"

"I wouldn't know about Gucci cologne."

Next, Dița teases out a bundle of delicate twigs dotted with tiny oval seeds. "For digestion, asthma, bronchitis, even cancer."

"How do you know all this?" says Angela.

"From books. I've got lots. In a box." She looks towards our bookshelf, scanning titles left to right for anything of interest.

I sniff the bundle of twigs. "I know this smell, what is it?"

"If you know, why do you ask?" says Dița. "Wild cumin, that is."

"Cumin grows in our forest?"

"All sorts, if you know where to look."

Angela brings three steaming mugs of tea and I fetch a box of biscuits. Angela looks closer at the twigs on the table.

"Great, thank you, Dița. Cumin is very good in curry."

"Wouldn't know about that." Dița reaches for a mug and sips her drink. "Bergamot. This tea's got bergamot in it."

"Well spotted," says Angela.

"You're good, Dița," I add.

"They say I'm bad." She blows at her mug to cool the tea.

"Who's they?"

"People."

"Why?"

"They see me selling mushrooms. What they don't see, is me getting up at dawn in bad weather to go and find 'em. They don't see the bears and wild pigs that get in my way, neither."

"More bears?"

"I had to run away from a big one, last week. Dropped my best knife. I'll never find it." Dița sips her drink. "Quite nice, this."

Angela rises from her chair and opens a cupboard. She takes out a pack of tea and offers it to Dița. "Present, for you."

"*Mulțumesc.*" Dița eyes the label. "Who's this guy in the fancy coat?"

"Earl Grey," I say, "he was Britain's prime minister about two hundred years ago."

"Why is he on a packet of tea?"

"So people will buy it. I think he invented the blend, perhaps."

Diţa sniffs the pack of tea, puts it into her bag and rummages for something else. "Before I forget, here you are, Doamna."

She offers Angela another posy of bright green leaves and creamy white petals. Angela beams.

"These are lovely, thank you, Diţa, but you shouldn't, really."

"Jasmine, that is."

"Thought so." Angela passes the flowers to me. "Try that."

I sniff the petals. *Such scent.* "Jasmine? In our forest? Wow."

Diţa chuckles. "No, Domnul, I got those from a neighbour's garden. He told me to take some, so that's what I did."

"What's jasmine good for?" says Angela.

"All sorts," says Diţa. "Tea, for a start."

"Ah, yes, but what would *you* recommend?"

"Me?" Diţa pauses for a moment. She sits looking round and about, here and there, then points across the room. "I'd just stick 'em in that nice vase and enjoy 'em while I can, hah!"

Her cackling laughter rings around our rafters, and bright blue eyes glitter in her leathery face.

Trei Mușchetari

High-pitched voices echo down the lane, as my wife and I walk up it with our dogs. Ahead of us, three men are leaning against a fence, silhouetted against the morning sun, with sticks at their hips. They wear floppy sun hats, loose shirts, and baggy pants tucked into boots. The Three Musketeers on tea break? Even at fifty metres, we can hear them quite clearly. *Yap yap yap.*

These valleys are quite something. Sometimes, you'll hear folks chatting two hundred metres away, on the next hill. Often, shepherds on different hills will chat with each other across the little valley between them, voices barely raised. The breeze and natural acoustics combine to do the rest. *So, watch what you say.*

Our three musketeers are not discussing the politics of seventeenth-century France. They're wittering about water – a frequent subject up this end of the village but one that rarely leads to accord. Usually, it culminates in a fierce row and sometimes worse. Good job those sticks are not swords.

"There's Vasile and Iacob. Who's the other guy?" I ask.

Angela shrugs. "Hard to tell under that hat, but I think it's the little fellow who tries to sell you sticks. At inflated prices."

"Yup, it's what's-his-name. Longshanks."

"I wouldn't call him that. His real name is Vasile. Actually, I think people call him *Vasilică,* the diminutive form, to distinguish between him and the older Vasile. So, just say, *Vasilică.*"

"I have a better idea." I raise a thumb as we approach the trio of men. *"Bună ziua, Cei Trei Mușchetari."*

They stop chatting and turn towards us, drunk as lords. Iacob swishes the air with his stick as if it's a rapier. *En garde!* Dark hair curls from under his wide hat and his little beard is a tufty triangle. Eyes glassy with booze, his squint is worse than ever. *Some swordsman.*

Vasilică the Diminutive raises his long walking stick, holding it vertically for me to see. It's almost as big as he is. The shaft is carved with elaborate eye-catching swirls, for which numerous tourists down in Bran will pay a pretty penny, or so I've heard.

"How about this one, Domnul Mike?"

"Very nice, Vasilică."

"Just tell me when, Domnul Mike."

"I will, when you reduce your prices."

"Hah, this is English humour, I think."

But not very funny, I think, judging by Vasilică's despondent demeanour. *Then again, is he ever cheerful?* Not as far as I recall. Something infinitely sad about his rheumy gaze and rumpled air. Inside this particular shepherd is a frustrated artisan, perhaps.

The older fellow next to him, grey-haired Vasile thrusts a hand into a pocket. He seems to be searching for something. "Doamna Angela, greetings. I owe you money for water, for August."

"Not to mention June and July," says Angela.

"Really? Sorry, I forgot, Madam Treasurer."

"Never mind *Madam Treasurer.* If you want me to handle the money, I will, but please pay it on time. I told you last month. What if everyone *forgot?* How am I supposed to pay the electricity bill for the pump? Do we have a goose with a golden egg?"

"Doamna, if you want eggs, I've got lots."

"I'm fine, Vasile, thanks. Anyway, did you get my text?"

"Text?"

"I sent a text to everyone whose water comes from the spring. I asked for volunteers to empty and clean the concrete tanks, up there, before winter comes." Angela points at the tree-lined hills.

"Doamna Angela, you didn't send me a text. When?"

"Sunday afternoon, Vasile."

"No, you didn't. I can't read 'em."

He glances at his companions, tongue out. *Geddit?* They nod and chuckle, eyes like slits. *That's a good 'un.* But Iacob raises a finger. Ah, he remembers. "I got a text, Doamna, after church."

"So, why didn't you reply?" says Angela, friendly but firm.

Iacob caresses his little beard. "I didn't understand it."

"Which bit?"

"Well, all of it."

Vasile gives me a wink and taps his temple. *Thick, our Iacob.*

"What about you, Vasilică?" says Angela.

Vasilică stands with one foot on the fence, his thumbs tucked into his waistcoat, and his elegant stick in the crook of his arm. Watery blue eyes peep from the shadow under his hat. "Me?"

"Did you get my text?"

"Phone's on the blink. *Volunteers*, you say?"

"Yes, to clean the tanks. I asked twelve families. No reply."

"What did it say, this text of yours? The actual words?"

Angela pulls out her phone, pokes at the screen, and reads aloud. *"Dear Neighbours, we need three volunteers to drain and clean the water tanks. Please contact me if you can help. PS. August fees are due."*

She holds up her phone. Unseeing eyes stare from crusty, weather-beaten faces. Our tipsy neighbours resemble gargoyles. Never mind swashbuckling with rapiers, they should be perched on a medieval cathedral in Paris.

"Volunteers?" says grey-haired Vasile, with a buttery smirk. "You don't need volunteers. We'll do it, won't we lads?"

"Suppose we could," says Vasilică, clearly thrilled.

Curly-haired Iacob crouches to thrust his stick at a fence post. "All for one! Just say the word, Madam Treasurer."

"But refreshments might help?" adds Vasile.

"Very well," says Angela. "After the job is done, deal?"

We all shake hands. Vasile's grip is firm despite the absence of a thumb and finger. "Left them in a sawmill didn't I, Domnul Mike?"

"That must've hurt like hell."

"It did but not any more. Fancy a little glass?" He nods towards a house beyond the fence, where, presumably, hooch can be had. Iacob points with his stick. *In there, Domnul Mike.*

Angela and I make our excuses and move on. The dogs strain at their leashes, desperate for muddy ditches. Wind hisses rustles through the swaying birch trees. Behind us, The Three Musketeers are arguing about how to drain and clean the big cement tanks up at the spring.

What? Are you crazy, Iacob?

Angela looks worried as we stride along the lane. Not easy being *Madam Treasurer,* when nobody answers, reads, or even receives your texts. I nudge her arm.

"At least you got your volunteers for the water tanks."

"Imagine that."

"What's up?"

"They'll probably fall in."

King of the Mountain

I love these summer evenings in Transylvania when the only sound is the gentle clinking of cowbells. I love sitting on our wooden terrace, admiring the dark outline of mountains or reading a book. I feel lucky because here we have time to think and air to breathe. No pollution, no traffic, and no rush.

There is, however, a loud and insistent thumping at our door, as if someone needs rescuing from certain death. My watch says 22.45, and my wife's anxious glance says, *You go.* I close my book, rise, and head indoors.

Through the window in our lobby, I spy a large, middle-aged man standing outside. He's tall, barrel-chested, and disheveled. Half of his frayed shirt collar is turned up and his chunky jumper looks as though it was knitted with bargepoles. His thick blonde hair sprouts in different directions like a worn-out brush. He has a broad neck and square chin. Bulbous eyes stare at our glass panels, as if he senses a presence beyond but cannot see me in the gloom. A white plastic bag containing something spherical and heavy dangles from his wrist. *Ah, he's seen me.* He yanks at the door handle. It's locked. He bangs with a fist the size of a grapefruit. Perhaps he's come to beat me up.

"Domnul!" His voice is hoarse, his tone indignant. Angela calls from the terrace. "Mike, who is it?"

"Just a neighbour, don't worry."

"Which neighbour?"

"Guess."

"Not Petre?"

"The one and only. I think he's sloshed."

"What does he want at this time of night?"

"No idea, I'll ask."

I turn the key, but it sticks. *Great.* Petre hammers and bellows. *Let me in!* Perhaps he's found God and wants us to pray. Perhaps he's found a football and wants us to play. Perhaps he's lost his mind and wants to stay. You never know, with Petre. The key clicks and I twist the handle. Petre shoves the door open and steams into the lobby, immense and determined, a hungry bear in search of porridge. He seizes my arm. "We must talk!"

"Petre, do come in. Talk about what?"

A smile splits his leathery face. "I'm having a party."

"Tonight?"

"No, but soon. I'm here to invite you. Will you come? With Doamna Angela?"

"Yes, if we're free, thank you."

"Where's Doamna?"

Before I can answer, Petre lumbers past me. He pauses to kick off his stout boots – a thoughtful touch, given the apparent rush – and moves on.

"Doamna Angela, you look so nice!"

He kisses my wife's hand, and slides onto a chair at our dining table. *What a charmer.*

He's still with us an hour later, if Petre is ever actually *with* anyone. As usual, he's in a world of his own and rambling on, with a disarming naiveté, about whatever springs to mind: his military service, his costly turf lawn, half a cow that his friend Longshanks found partly buried by a bear who obviously planned to come back.

"Longshanks was quite worried because a bear will turn up when you least expect," says Petre, and he ain't kidding.

Since he doesn't listen much, it's hardly a friendly chat, more of a friendly monologue. Try to contribute and he'll ignore you, or nod in agreement and change the subject. He's harmless enough, I suppose, but over-friendly, even intimidating, at times. Your space is his space. He'll edge his chair ever closer, tap your arm three times and lean into you as he speaks. Petre has a good heart, mind you, a very good heart. We know this because he keeps telling us. He spreads his sausage fingers and slaps his chest, like Tarzan, or an affable Apache: *Me Good Heart.*

On the other hand, we know that our good-hearted neighbour drives his old blue truck rather recklessly, rants and raves in his yard, stresses his elderly mother, and is currently relishing his hard-won status as King of the Mountain, whatever that means. Something to do with grazing rights and a bidding war, which Petre won by fair means or foul. We've heard rumours of sheepduggery up the hill, although envy is often the default psychological setting among mountain people. Or so we've been told by self-confessed, non-envious, good-hearted mountain people.

There's something else that we know about Petre: his failed romance, the marriage that didn't happen. He has never mentioned it and we'll never ask, but then again, we don't need to, seeing as it's still one of the most popular topics of conversation in the village, at least when Petre is not in earshot. Perhaps he's put it all behind him, moved on, and forgiven those who wrecked his dream of a happy life with a wife and kids. I doubt it, somehow.

Petre sits back, gazing at our paintings. "Nice place, this."

"Thanks," says Angela, "more tea?"

"No, but perhaps a beer with you, Domnul Mike?"

"Sorry, Petre, we're out."

"Got any *țuică?*" He twiddles his thumbs and gives me a fiendish grin. Such a request is rarely refused. Everyone has hooch, in these hills. He rises slowly to his feet and goes to peruse the magnets on our fridge; the little red London bus impresses him, although our miniature Picasso does not. Angela seems uneasy but gives me the nod: *țuică, whatever.*

I pour two shot glasses. The potent brew shimmers and shines in the candlelight. "You'll like this, Petre. Great flavour. Made from grapes. Angela's dad–"

"I've got a fridge like that, only bigger."

"Cheers, here's to your fridge."

We clink and drink. Fridge-upmanship, there's a new one. Petre drains his glass in one gulp. "Not bad, but mine's better."

"You mentioned a party?" says Angela.

Petre smacks his lips and returns to his seat. "Plums. You should use plums."

"Petre?"

"Yes, Doamna?"

"You mentioned a party."

"Right. I'm here to invite you. Will you come? We've been working hard to organise it, me and Longshanks, that is."

"When is it?"

"Friday, and Saturday, and probably Sunday, God willing."

"Three days? What's the occasion?"

"The occasion, Doamna?" Our garrulous visitor seems momentarily lost for words. He nudges his empty glass across the table, in case I haven't noticed. "Actually, my party is to celebrate my new house. Bigger than this one."

"We know, we've seen it."

"But have you been inside, Doamna? No, I don't think so. It's a palace, you'll see."

I refill Petre's glass. "To your new house."

"New house!" Petre gulps his hooch and stands up. "Must go, Domnul."

"So soon?" I ask. Angela's foot nudges mine. Petre peeps under the table. Our timing is unfortunate but he seems not to notice.

"Almost forgot, Doamna, brought you this."

He swings the plastic bag onto the table and invites us to admire the contents – a spherical white cheese, the size of a football.

Angela lifts the bag. "Wow, this must weigh three kilos. Thank you, Petre, but really there's no need to give–"

"Think I can't afford it? Well, I can. So, don't you worry about me, Doamna, ок?"

For once, Petre's tone is off. Bitterness lurks beneath the bonhomie. I tap his arm, dead matey. "She didn't mean it that way."

"Then what does she m-mean, Domnul?" His speech is slurred and his eyes are bloodshot. He stares at me, and then at Angela, who pats his forearm, *there-there*.

"I meant you're very generous, Petre, and everyone says so."

"Who's everyone?"

"People in the village, your friends."

"Because I have a good heart." He places a huge hand on his chest. "God knows I have."

I move to the door. "Very true, Petre, and thanks for the invite, see you at the party."

"Wait, look at this, just so you know."

He reaches back, as though pulling a pistol from his belt for a showdown. Instead, he produces a thick wad of folded banknotes and thrusts it towards us.

"Look at this, see what I've got?"

We look and we see. He's got five thousand lei, easy. That's what, €1,000? He licks a gnarled thumb and peels back cash, with the fond regard of a proud father whose babies are banknotes.

"See this, Domnul Mike? This is *nothing*. I'm rich, richer than anyone in this village because I work from dawn until dusk. Always did. I work hard. God knows I work hard."

He's not smiling anymore; he's defiant and daring us to disagree. But we don't, and he lurches away, groping for the door and wobbling down the steps, arms outstretched for balance.

"Careful, Petre," says Angela, "you're carrying a lot of cash, better not lose it."

"*Lose it?* Hah, and what if I do, Doamna? Plenty more where this came from. So, yes, I can afford to give you a little chunk of cheese, and I hope you like it. You won't taste better. Look at those stars, will you? Look, up there!"

Angela and I obey, craning our necks as Petre zig-zags into the darkness. We watch him go, *bye Petre.* We watch him trot back to us. He's giggling like a kid, quite a transformation from the belligerent grown-up who just departed. "Forgot my boots!"

I hand them over and Petre carries one in each hand, oblivious to any sharp stones underfoot, as he makes his way towards his house, thirty metres up the lane, where a scrawny silhouette appears at a window. His poor mother.

Preparations for the party begin on Monday morning with the laying of turf. From our kitchen window, we watch workmen rolling out strips of bright green grass, and village kids offering advice.

By mid-afternoon, a lush lawn has replaced the muddy gravel in Petre's yard. His elderly mother stands watching as the final sods are pressed into place. She's wearing a blue housecoat, and her customary black headscarf for a husband long gone. She spots us passing with our dogs, and walks towards her front gate for a chat. She swings her arms in wide arcs, as though speed skating. Deep wrinkles crease her face as she smiles. "Hey, you two, seen this lovely lawn? Don't pretend you didn't."

Angela raises a thumb. "Lovely lawn, Tanti Lina."

"Petre paid. Cost him a fortune. Such a good boy. Out with your dogs again? Every day, walk-walk. Do they pay you? No. You should work, Domnul Mike."

"We do work, Tanti Lina."

"Doing what, I'd like to know. You need to buy some sheep. At least a cow. If you don't work, you don't eat. Are you coming to our party? Petre said you weren't sure. You *must* come! There'll be food, music, and dancing. He's invited half the village. But not *everyone*, of course."

Tanti Lina narrows her eyes and looks up the lane towards her neighbours' house, fifty metres away among tall firs. I track her gaze and spot two people – a man and woman, probably Domnul Tudor and his young wife Mirela – chatting in the shade of the trees. Something silver glints between them. Tudor's motorbike? Yes, he's standing alongside it and turning the handlebars, left and right. I glance back at Tanti Lina. Her mouth is set in a grimace. She's probably wondering why pretty, vivacious Mirela ended up with Tudor, instead of with big-hearted, hard-working Petre.

After a few moments of deafening silence, Tanti Lina wishes us well and walks back to her lovely lawn. To my eye, it's looking a bit higgledy-piggledy, but will no doubt settle down in time. Things usually do.

Over the next few days, several more workmen arrive to help prepare for Petre's big night. They erect steel poles for a marquee, unload trestle tables from a truck, and lay long planks on a section of the new lawn.

"Dance floor," a tired-looking fellow in a pork pie hat tells us. It seems an odd idea, considering new turf needs sunlight, fresh air, and probably water. When I mention this, he just shrugs.

"You're quite right, but Petre wants lots of dancing, so we have to make this."

A job is a job, and a party is a party, after all.

The saxophones kick off, loud and proud, at eight o'clock on Friday morning, while we're having breakfast. The tune echoes down the lane from Petre's yard to our house. It's fast and furious, twisting and turning. If an eel on amphetamines could write music, it would sound like this. A singer joins in, his sorrowful voice heavy on the melodrama. He sounds as if he's pleading for his life before a firing squad. Angela cocks an ear and tells me that, no, the song is about how much he adores his elusive sweetheart. We listen with worried faces, partly for her and partly for ourselves – three days and nights of this stuff?

It's traditional Romanian *muzică populară*, the sort that makes you want to dance a jig or bury your head under a pillow, depending on your mood. I find it intriguing and irritating in equal measure because such musicians are talented, technically proficient, and have seemingly limitless stamina, but every song sounds the same, has a repetitive structure, and lasts about twenty minutes. Angela stirs a spoon around her coffee, in slow circles. "Bit early to be playing a CD this loud, don't you think?"

"It's not a CD. Sounds more like a live band, warming up."

She walks to the kitchen window and looks out. "You're right. I can see two men playing saxophones in Petre's marquee. What a din. I doubt you'll do much work today. Looks like Petre's mate Longshanks is up there as well, bossing people about. What time should we arrive tonight, nine?"

"Nine-ish. What will you wear, a nice dress?"

"And earplugs, otherwise I'll be deaf by ten."

Come party time, Angela selects a dress of yellow, grey, and red rectangles. It's like a painting by Mondrian, very elegant. I'm wearing dark trousers and a shirt of spiralling blue spots; it's from Down Under, if rather over the top. We put on our nicest shoes and walk up the muddy lane, sidestepping discs of fresh cow kak.

Petre's place looks lovely. The neat borders of the lush lawn are lit with flickering torches, and white fairy lights sparkle like glow-worms around the dance floor. Male guests – five named Tudor, four named Mihai, three named Radu, and two named Ioan – stand around in tight groups, chatting away. Some of them tease a fellow who sports a bright yellow waistcoat, although to be fair, he looks very smart. Wives and girlfriends cluster around Petre's tall and beautiful sister Gloria, admiring her posh frock. They're all dressed to the tens in heels and hats, sipping from long glasses: *Sănătate! Your health!*

Hanging baskets perfume the warm air and candles glow along elaborately-laid tables, where older guests sit eyeing the fruit and cheese. Waiters and waitresses in neat black and white uniforms glide back and forth, to and from the house. Young girls skip about in satin ballgowns. A little boy in a bow tie strokes a timid-looking three-legged dog that wags its stubby tail, happy to be invited.

Tanti Lina greets us with kisses, *mwah*. She's wearing a brown housecoat with pink piping, and a black headscarf with turquoise paisley motif – it's party time, after all. She asks me whether I want a nice three-legged dog – *Just kidding, Domnul Mike!* – then veers away to scold a dozy waiter. Angela nudges my arm and murmurs, "There's your pal Longshanks, doing the rounds."

"All dressed up, too. I hardly recognise him." I watch tiny, rheumy-eyed Longshanks ambling around the guests. He's wearing a boxy suit with two-inch turn-ups and carrying a beer bottle in each hand. He waves one at me, doing his best to smile. He's heading our way. I turn to my wife, with an urgent question.

"Angela, quick, tell me again, what's Longshanks' real name? I can never remember."

"Vasile. Or you can use *Vasilică*, the diminutive. He might like that, it's less formal."

"I don't think he likes anything, much. Why does he always look so miserable, even in summer?"

"Perhaps he has an allergy."

"To what? Life in general?"

"Maybe you should ask him. In a polite way."

But Longshanks, aka Vasilică, gets ambushed, en route to us, by a chatty lady en route to him. She's asking directions. He points one of his beer bottles at the house, and the other at me. *With you in a moment.* I watch and wait. Must remember to greet him by his proper name. *Longshanks* sounds like a schoolyard joke.

"Angela, how come half the men here are named Vasile?"

"Because the other half are called Tudor or Radu."

"That's three halves."

"Welcome to Culmea. Maria's waving. Must mingle."

Angela moves away and Longshanks strolls up, offering me a dusty bottle.

"Beer, Domnul Mike?"

"No thanks, Vasile. *Vasilică*, I mean. I'll get some wine from a waiter."

"Suit yourself." He tilts his head back and swigs away, gazing at purple sky. I can see right up his hairy nostrils. He smacks his lips. "So, you like our turf?"

"Looks great, Vasilică, lovely lawn."

"I should've brought my sheep."

We chat about his sheep, his cows, the risk of drought, and, inevitably, about his walking sticks.

"Made some beauties recently, Domnul Mike, long and strong. You should buy one."

"I have several sticks, already. Radu Moraru gave me one. Tudor Banică, too. And Ioan Nicolae. So, thanks, Longshanks, but I'm fine. *Vasilică*, I mean. Fine for sticks, that is, walking sticks."

He tugs my sleeve and gazes up, all weepy-eyed like a homeless goblin. "Domnul Mike."

"Yes, Vasilică?"

"You told me last time we met, about Moraru and all the rest. But I've seen their sticks. Do they carve the shaft? No! Mine look better, and I fit a nice brass cap at the end to protect the wood."

"You said that last time, too."

"Because it's true. Carved stick with a brass cap, you need. If you had one of mine, you'd look like a real shepherd."

"With no sheep."

"I could sell you a few."

"My wife would be thrilled."

"So, that's a good reason. How many?"

"Fifty."

"Surely you are not serious?"

"Correct."

"Hah, English humour. Where's your sweet wife?"

"Chatting with what's-her-name in the hat, see?"

"That's my Tanti Maria, who just pretends to be sweet."

"Doamna Maria is your auntie? I never knew that."

"There's lots you don't know, Domnul."

"Such as?"

"How much Petre spent on this party. He has a good heart."

"That much I do know."

"Talk of the devil," says Vasilică, with a wink, and our genial host appears on the lawn, wearing a black silk shirt, black leather waistcoat, black jeans and shiny black boots with Cuban heels. All he needs is a black Stetson and a six-gun. He makes a beeline towards Angela for a *how-do-you-hug*, then yanks her by the wrist, across the lawn. I watch with interest.

"Petre wants her to see his house," says Vasilică, "you should see it too, a palace. Come and look, follow me."

We walk across the lawn and into the house. Big Petre is barging around the wide, tiled lobby and pointing through various doors. Nervous-looking waitresses slip out of his way.

"Kitchen is here," says Petre, "d'you like it, Doamna Angela? With my fridge, didn't I tell you? And look, here's the dining room, and through there is the lounge. So, what do you say?"

He sounds as if he's hoping Angela might buy the place. I catch a few knowing smiles among the other guests nosing around. Perhaps everyone gets The Tour.

"Very nice," says Angela.

Petre grabs her arm. "The bedrooms!" Angela totters on her heels as Petre hauls her upstairs.

Vasilică beckons me to follow, and on the first floor, we glimpse yet more wonders – several bedrooms with *en-suite* bathrooms, double beds, little tables, reading lamps, wardrobes, and cupboards. Everywhere smells of sawn wood and fresh paint, but the floor has a distinct slope. It's a bit like The Haunted House in a fun fair. Either that, or we're sinking fast.

Petre thumps my bicep. "Hey, it's Domnul Mike!"

We all go downstairs and back onto the lawn, where Petre drapes his arms around our necks and urges us to have a good time. "But now forgive me, I must start the dancing." He strides towards the marquee, where red-shirted musicians are in full swing.

"Time for a drink," says Angela, and I won't disagree. We follow our host through the canvas awning.

The band is blasting *muzică populară*. Two ruddy-faced saxophonists weave riddle-diddle runs with nimble fingers, the keyboard player pokes chords and bass lines, synthesised drums boom from humungous speakers, and a tubby male singer serenades the tables of beaming guests. He wears a white tuxedo and is dabbing his eyes with a white hanky. He's either besotted with his sweetheart or boiling to death. A smiling waiter offers us glasses of wine from a painted wooden tray. "White for Doamna? Red for Domnul?"

Cheers, don't mind if we do.

We watch Petre lead half a dozen little kids in a merry romp around the wooden planks – he's the life and soul of the party, with funny faces to make them giggle. No wonder they're always loitering in his yard. Petre scoops up a tiny boy and twirls him around and around. Quite the gentle giant, sometimes.

"How's your wrist?" I ask my wife.

"A bit sore, he wouldn't let go. I suppose he's just happy. Was it three bedrooms or four? I lost count."

"Five, and a dodgy floor. I felt like I was on the Titanic. Who built that house?"

"Someone who shouldn't. Poor Petre," Angela shakes her head.

Eager guests shimmy to the dance floor and soon the joint is creaking. Angela extracts a fly from her glass. "How was Longshanks, did he try to sell you a stick?"

"And some sheep, which is new."

"What did you say?"

"I told him we need fifty."

"Good. You'll need a hut, too, when you move out."

"How was Tanti Maria?"

Angela leans closer. "She told me Mirela is an ungrateful tart and Tudor's house is very small."

"As in very flat?"

"Don't be mean. What do you think?"

"Mirela is very nice. And size isn't everything."

Petre and the kids form a ring and he leads them in a slowly-rotating *hora*, all smiles. He'd make a great dad, if and when he gets over his broken heart. I gaze up the lane towards the next house, the small one between the fir trees. The lights are on and everyone's home. Tudor and Mirela can hear this barnstorming band, no problem, and if they cared to peep out, they could probably see Petre dancing. But what they can't do, is walk down and join in. Nor would they want to. And everyone here knows why.

"What are you thinking?" says Angela.

"About the course of true love. Fancy a dance?"

"You asking?"

"I'm asking."

"I'm dancing, after this drink." She touches her wine glass against mine. "First summer in Culmea."

"Home sweet home, lucky we're here."

To the west, the jagged limestone ridge of Piatra Craiului looks as sharp as shark's teeth. To the east, the dusky Bucegi Mountains guard their ancient secrets. It's midsummer in Transylvania and I'll drink to that.

After an hour of bopping in stiff shoes, I need a break. Angela agrees, so we vacate the planks and sit at a table. Angela chats with a trio of well-dressed ladies and I've got a cheery, freckle-faced redhead for company. Turns out Domnul Daniel shares my interest in football and is a big fan of Steaua Bucharest – no surprises there. Eventually, he pops the question.

"Who'll win the Premiership, Domnul Mike?"

"Not Liverpool, Domnul Daniel, not this year."

The truth hurts but the food compensates, and we munch away, huddled elbow-to-elbow. The local cheese is excellent – creamy with a tang – and the fried carp breaks easily from the bone. Daniel pours me a glass of *țuică,* and we take turns toasting our favourite footballers, such as Hagi the legendary Romanian and Dalglish the legendary Scotsman. Daniel tells me there are lots more but I blow the whistle after our second glass, lest I end up being carried off the field of play on a stretcher.

"Domnul Mike," says Daniel, "sometimes I wonder, when passing your house, why do you live in our village?"

Sometimes I wonder where to start. Perhaps with an olive.

"Because it's nice, Daniel, don't you think?"
He looks to the darkening hills. "I suppose so."

The King of the Mountain is seriously displeased when we decide to leave his court. He spots us bidding our goodbyes and marches cross the lawn, which is looking rather worse for wear, just like him. Swaying, he blocks our exit. "Doamna Angela, where d'you think you're going?"

"Home, Petre, it was a great party, thank you."

He seizes her wrist. She tries to move away, but he won't let go. "Doamna Angela, you didn't dance."

"Yes, I did, Petre, quite a lot, actually."

"Not with me you didn't, only with Domnul."

"Petre, it's four in the morning. We're tired."

"So? It's the weekend. My party's just starting. It will last all of today and Sunday too, God willing."

"So there's plenty of time, yes? Perhaps we'll come back and I'll dance with you, if you're free. But perhaps you'll have lots of partners, like tonight."

"Doamna, I'll be free, you can count on it. So, come back. Tomorrow, anytime, I insist. Bring Domnul, too."

It sounds like an offer we can't refuse, and maybe we won't. But we do depart, stepping carefully down the lane towards home, under a black sky and a billion stars.

The band is tooting away and its repetitive music must be audible for miles around. Good luck to anyone abed and trying to sleep, in these hills. Then again, most people in these hills are not abed. They're at Petre's party. Because he has a good heart.

On our short walk home, we pass another guest. I recognise the yellow waistcoat and white jeans, although until now I had not noticed the hole in the sole of his boot. He's on his back in the field opposite our house. *Dead, or dead drunk?* Time will tell. Five brown cows stand around him in a semi-circle, chewing. One turns her huge, silken head towards us and the brass bell jangles on her collar. She has beautiful big eyes, with a glimmer of sadness, as ever. *How now?* I slide my key into the lock on our gate. Our dogs wobble from their musty kennels to welcome us with yawns and waggy tails. *What time do you call this, folks?* Bed time, is what.

Sleep, however, does not come easily. Fact is, it doesn't come at all. Our bed is soft and comfy, but my ears are roaring and I can still hear music blasting away up the lane. I check my watch – 05.45 – and roll onto my side. Dawn fills our room with its golden glow. How inspiring. Perhaps I'll get up and craft pretty verses, like Wordsworth. Or maybe I'll just lie here with poet's block.

"You still awake, Mike?"

"No, Angela, I'm fast asleep. How about you?"

"Not a wink. Music's too loud." Angela folds an arm behind her head, and points. "We've got a spider."

"And a party for the next twenty-fours, at least. God willing."

"I feel a bit sorry for him, to be honest."

"The spider? So do I, this noise must do his web in."

"I mean Petre."

"Because?"

Angela turns towards me. "I heard some bad stuff."

"Apart from the music, you mean?"

"Stuff about Petre and Mirela, their romance."

"Failed romance. She's history book, end of."

"You don't know the half of it."

"Such as?"

"What went on between her, Petre, and Tudor."

"That's three halves. Welcome to Culmea."

"Are you going to listen or not?"

"Shoot, I'm all tinnitus."

"It seems Tanti Lina and Petre had a few disagreements. About the new house, about the auction for grazing rights on the mountain, even about Mirela."

"Before or after Petre proposed to her?"

"That's just it. Seems he didn't. No ring, no announcement, so no one knows. What they do know is, he built that big house for Mirela and planned this party for their engagement."

"Alleged engagement. Who broke it off?"

"Not clear, but Mirela fell for Tudor in the meantime. So, now, we're just celebrating Petre's new house."

"Alleged house."

"I feel sorry for all three of them. Imagine having a whole village yapping about your private life?"

"The soup thickens and don't friends love to stir it."

"I'd move away. Private life is private, after all."

"I just had an idea. We could start a radio station. *Gossip FM: All The Mud That Will Stick.* Imagine the advertising revenue, from sheep dip manufacturers."

"Nobody dips sheep around here." Angela points at the ceiling. "Where's the spider gone?"

"To the party for a dance."

She slumps back onto her pillow. Birds flutter at our window. Clever ones. Building sticky nests under our eaves. Up and down, back and forth, *flappity-flap.*

"Did you know, Angela, house martins sleep while they fly? Ten thousand feet up, migrating from Africa,

89

and they nod off. Or was it swifts? Anyway, they invented auto-pilot. My brother told me, he has house martins, too."

"Very interesting. I wonder if house martins can sleep during a disco? I wish Petre would turn the music down."

"You should count spiders. Probably hundreds in here."

"Thanks a lot. You know the worst I heard?"

"Singer in the white tux. We'll play his CDs on *Gossip FM*."

"Never mind him. Something about Petre."

"There is something about Petre, agreed."

"It seems that he's been very depressed, recently."

"Petre, depressed? That's a good 'un."

"He was telling people that his heart is broken and there is nothing to live for. Tanti Lina took him to see the priest."

"Cheaper than a shrink, I suppose. *Oh, what a tangled web.* Anyway, he's not depressed now. He's enjoying himself, so we shouldn't begrudge him this party. Let's count spiders."

"Poor Petre. I hope he finds someone else."

"Poor, with that fistful of dollars?"

We lie side by side, wondering about our not-so-poor neighbour, in silence. Sort of.

We rise at noon and breakfast on our terrace, gazing at the mountains and enjoying the blissful quiet, broken only by our munching of muesli and the tinkle of distant cowbells. But all too soon, the din starts in the marquee, and we opt to walk the dogs, over the hills and far away, lest we go bonkers.

Ambling up our lane, we see no sign of Petre, just ten newcomers who seem thrilled to be in his yard, quaffing beers and nodding to the music. It must be a CD, because there's no band, just two morose-looking lads in woolly jumpers and jeans who sit on stools near the low stage, half-heartedly tooting their saxophones, warming up for their own performance later, no doubt. They lack the sartorial style of last night's lounge lizards, but they're here on time. Petre must have hired them to take over and entertain his happy hordes. Somehow, I doubt we'll be among them.

The party lasts all day, all night, and ends around 10 a.m. on Sunday, since even God needs a day off. When the sax players riddle their last riff, Angela and I are lurching around our house like zombies in need of a kill. Call me old-fashioned, but a party that long was too long, especially as it offered no chill-out zone for guests and no respite for local residents. I bet even Mexican drug barons pull the plug after twenty-four hours of celebrations. They've got jobs, after all.

I'm stumbling towards next winter's woodpile, to secure some wobbly logs, when a familiar voice rasps at me from the lane. "Domnul Mike!"

"Morning, Petre." I try to sound friendly but I've hardly slept for forty-eight hours thanks to his *muzică populară,* at nose-bleed volume. All is quiet now, but I'm tight-headed and skittish. It feels like jet lag, minus helpful air miles and goodies from duty-free. Instead, I've got chores. And now Petre, who doesn't look in the least depressed. He looks impatient, beckoning me to the fence. "Come, see."

"See what, Petre?"

"Just come, Domnul Mike, please, it's very important."

A few minutes later, I'm sitting on a wobbly wooden stool in Petre's glittering kitchen, and poring over a box of his old photos. He's standing beside me, pouring two glasses of chilled, homemade rosé. *Am I dreaming?* I'm past caring. We clink glasses, but not to his fuck-you-fridge. We're toasting our friendship, at 10.30.

Petre brandishes photo after photo, explaining who's who and where was when. *Domnul Mike, here's me aged nine, and here's Longshanks on his horse, and here's me in the army, and here's more wine.* Petre's life story is a bit of a blur, but the plonk is decent, even irresistible. *Am I going native?* Seems like it. *Will Petre ever shut up?* Seems not. I'll have cirrhosis of the ears, soon.

A worried-looking lad in dungarees enters the room, clutching a pen and a folded sheet of paper. He offers the paper to Petre.

"Please Domnul, check my sums?"

The lad offers the pen as well, but Petre ignores it, unfolds the sheet of paper and places it on the table. I see a long list of items with numbers alongside and a total at the bottom. Petre leans over it, reading silently to himself, opening and closing his mouth like a stranded fish. He takes the pen, amends the total, and refolds the paper. "Wrong by twenty lei. Be more careful."

The lad pockets the paper and backs out of the room. He looks scared to death but servitude is alive and well. "Yes, Domnul. Sorry, Domnul."

Petre pulls a wad of cash from his pocket and holds it up. We've been here before, even if I haven't been here before. Maybe this time, I'll ask Willy Wonga for a loan to buy some sheep, a hut, and a walking stick with a brass cap. Longshanks would weep for joy.

"See this money, Domnul Mike? See what this means, my friend? Means I'm rich. Because I work hard, God knows I do. But the thing is, I'm careful, too, and that's also very important. Because you have to watch the numbers, always. But, please, forgive the interruption. Where were we?"

"You were in the army, aged twenty."

"Guess how old I am now?"

"About forty-five?"

"Forty-eight! I look younger, yes?" His hoarse voice rises in delight. I can only agree, and wonder when I'll be de-mobbed. Petre refills my glass with homemade rosé. No time soon, then.

Summer rolls on and Petre disappears for a bit. He's probably up his mountain, doing whatever kings do. I can't say I miss his roaring truck or loud arguments with Tanti Lina, but life is less interesting, somehow, when he's not around. So, I'm not displeased when I spot him, about a month later, ambling up our lane. I am curious, however, because he looks different – stooped and skinnier, half the man I knew. His shoulders seem almost bony under his flannel shirt. He's with loyal little Longshanks, who seems to have grown, in comparison. They each carry a long-handled *coasă,* and appear worn out after a hard day's scything.

I'm five metres way, crouched in our yard and tugging stubborn weeds from a border. I raise a hand in greeting but the two friends seem not to notice. Too tired, probably. Actually, they look rather worried. *Should I offer them a drink of water?* No point, really,

Petre's house is very close and if he invites me over there to see something important, I might end up sleeping on my back in a field, surrounded by curious cows. So, I yank another weed and watch them dawdle up the road. *What a pair, Little & Large.*

They pause briefly at Petre's gate, then Longshanks continues alone up the lane. Petre enters his yard and flings his scythe across the lawn. It lands with a clatter. I suppose the party's long over and work has resumed, but even so, it's puzzling behaviour. Don't hill folk treasure those vital tools, and spend a long time beating their blades to keep them straight?

Next day, Petre is out scything with his sister Gloria, and Tanti Lina, in their field just across the lane. The two women seem in good spirits, chatting as they swish and swipe at the grass. They slice it cleanly into neat piles as they go. They make the work seem effortless, but such technique takes many summers of hard practice to perfect. I know, because my own attempts are usually risible in comparison.

As for Petre, he's working on his own, keeping a distance. *Aren't they all supposed to work in a team, side by side, and move across the land together?* Apparently not. Petre ignores their banter and keeps his head down as he turns and swings, shaving the slope like a man possessed.

The scorching summer stretches to mid-September, but by the end of the month, the wind is up and temperatures are down. Change is in the air, and about time too. Our little village needs rain. The communal water spring won't gush forever, and there have been droughts in years past, up that desiccated hill, or so I hear.

I'm listening to the weather forecast on the radio and Angela is outside, chatting with someone at our gate. When she comes in, she's clutching a plate of cakes wrapped in clingfilm.

"Doamna Dorina brought us these and some interesting news. Her daughter-in-law Mirela is pregnant."

"That was quick."

"I'll say. Dorina is thrilled, it's her first grandchild. But we mustn't tell Tanti Lina, in case she gets upset, what with Mirela being Petre's ex."

"My lips are sealed. My ears are wide open."

"You taking the dogs out?"

"In about two minutes, why?"

"Wear a coat. Looks like rain. I'll stay home, catch up on some emails, ok?"

"No problem."

I'm reaching for the dogs' leashes when my phone rings. The screen says *Radu Banică*, and Radu Banică says, "Domnul Mike, you walking your dogs today?"

Talk about a mindreader. Our neighbour from over the hill could probably bend our spoons if he wanted. *Radu Geller.*

"Yes, Radu, I'm leaving now, actually. Why?"

"Better not. Petre is bringing three hundred head of sheep down from the mountain, back to their owners. They'll be coming to the top field, end of your lane, quite soon I reckon."

"No problem, my dogs will be on leashes."

"But Petre's won't and he's got half a dozen."

"Dogs?"

"Huge ones. If they see your dogs, they'll kill 'em. Just saying. Up to you, but I'd skip the walk today."

"Maybe I will, thanks for the tip."

"Cu plăcere. See you."

The dogs seem displeased when I hang up their leashes. Sam cocks her six-inch ears: *Something I dug?* Linda sinks to the ground, deflated. *Bugger this.*

Then again, just because they can't go out doesn't mean I can't. After all, I'm not a dog. And I've never seen the annual sheep drive. Plus, six huge mutts? Too good to miss. So, I tell Angela, and walk alone up the lane. Our dogs yip and yelp at me from the yard: *What about us, you bastard?* The wind gets sharper and colder with every step and their howls soon fade.

At the top of the lane, I find Longshanks, aka Vasilică the diminutive, huddled in a brown felt waistcoat and leaning on a fence. A beautifully-carved walking stick is propped under his arm. I bet he'll try and flog it to me, once he spots the plain one in my hand, any second now. *Domnul Mike!*

But, no, Vasilică seems unmoved by my arrival. I get only a cursory nod. He looks even more fed up than usual, as though he's been weeping all night. I won't ask why. Nearby, grizzled shepherds mooch about in fleecy coats and rubber boots. Three curly-horned rams stare at me with eyes like button holes. So much for *three hundred head of sheep*. And where are the six huge dogs? I spy only two. Massive enough, mind you. They sprawl on the grass and are not the sort of pooches you might tempt with tidbits. These are the real deal – surly Transylvanian sheepdogs, fifty or sixty kilos apiece – that relish a midnight scrap with a bear and would eat our dogs for starters. The black one nearest the fence lifts its huge head to stare at me. I look away.

Vasilică wipes his eyes. I dip in my pocket and offer him a paper tissue. His brief smile exudes silent gratitude – *mulțumesc* – but he looks pretty rough.

"Morning, Vasilică. So, when will the sheep arrive?"

He parps his nose into the tissue. "Not today."

"Oh, how come? Petre changed his plans?"

"Petre is gone."

"Gone where?"

"He's dead, Domnul Mike, Petre is dead."

"What?"

Vasilică puts a hand at his neck, makes a fist, and yanks it towards his ear.

I gawp at him. "Petre *hung* himself?"

"Yes, Domnul Mike. In my house, last night. I came home and found him strung up in my living room. But don't tell his mama. We're saying it was his heart. But it wasn't, God forgive him. He told me he'd do it. I thought he was just fed up. I should've listened."

Vasilică sobs into his weather-beaten hands. The big dogs look up. A burly shepherd leads Vasilică away. Another shepherd joins them, offering a hip flask.

I stand alone for ten minutes, numb. Then I walk back down the lane, in a daze. *Petre hung himself? Last night?* It's beyond belief. Our big, brash, bombastic King of the Mountain, the kiddies' favourite and the loudest man in the village. Gone.

The wind claws my face and my brimming eyes sting. All too soon, bad memories come flitting through my brain like demented bats. I glimpse the blurred faces of two other friends who chose the same way out, back in the UK: Mick the failed footballer who turned to crime, and Gavin the workaholic DJ who was up until the dawn of crack. Dead and gone, both. *Now Petre as well?* I'm floating home, trying in vain to make any sense of it. Vasilică was correct, in one regard: you blame yourself for missing the signs. But would our friends have listened to us in their moment of need? I'm not so sure. When we pity these dear departed, do we miss the point? What if they did not want our pity? What if all they wanted was to escape the unspeakable and shake off the unbearable? What if something dazzled them in their darkness and offered hope? What if, in the end, they saw a new beginning?

I remember something else, too: a few weeks before they drifted away, both Mick and Gavin showed me fat wads of rolled cash, just like Petre did, as if to prove something. *See what this means, my friend?* No, I don't, because I can't. First, I have to wipe my eyes.

I steal a glance at distant mountains. They're silent, majestic, and eternal. Not fragile, like a man who would reign over them.

How to Build a Fence

We need a new fence around our big, grassy yard. A proper fence, one that our dogs cannot jump over, or wriggle through, in search of skittish sheep and stroppy donkeys. What we don't need, obviously, is one of these rough and rustic fences so popular around here. Because that's what we have now and it leans at a precarious angle, cross bars askew and ancient posts cracked, ready to topple in the next storm. I point through our window at it.

"We need a real fence out there, Angela."

"Agreed."

"So we can let the dogs run free."

"Exactly."

We gaze at our two hounds. They're chained to iron hoops and look bored witless. Angela thumbs her phone. "I'll ask Domnul Ionică, he's due next week. We'll add it to his list of jobs."

"Sooner the better. Tell him *seven bars high.*"

"Why seven bars?"

"My lucky number and too high for the dogs. Did you reserve rooms for Ionică and his sons?"

"Yes, in a local guest house. Hush, while I text him."

I sip coffee in silence. It feels good to be decisive for a change. To know what you want. Get things done.

Who'd have thought I'd end up in Transylvania? Funny how things turn out. I drain my drink and look at the logo on the old mug: BBC. If not for the BBC, I wouldn't even be in Romania. But that's another story. Today's top line is: *New Fence to Prevent Attacks on Sheep.*

Domnul Ionică and his sons Filip and Romeo arrive from Bucharest in their big white van. They climb out and unfurl the back flap. We peep inside. If Aladdin drove a truck, it would look like this – packed with goodies. Our trusty handymen have brought everything they need for our various renovations: drums of paint, electric saws, rusty drills, trusty toolboxes, snaky cables, sheets of polystyrene that resemble giant slices of bread, and plastic pots of who-knows-what. Angela and I help to unload dozens of small cardboard cartons that rattle, tubes of sticky-icky, balls of twine, sacks of cement, sacks of something else, and dustbin-sized rolls of thermal wool – the sort that makes your skin itch and is probably giving me cancer just looking at it.

Ionică seems tired after his five-hour drive. He stands to one side, dressed in scarlet overalls and puffing on a cigarette. His combover wafts up and down – a miniature magic carpet – in the mountain breeze. *Why not just go bald gracefully?* He mutters instructions to his sons, about what should go where. Handsome young Romeo is as quiet as ever, heaving and hauling the stuff, but Filip seems to relish his role as Deputy Dad; his hair is thinning too, making him seem older than his years. *He's what, thirty at most?*

"No, Mike, bring my toolbox over here, please."

"Sorry, Filip. Did you bring any timber for our fence?"

"No, Mike."

Filip's reply doesn't surprise me. In fact, if I had a dollar for every *No, Mike,* over the years we've known each other, I could buy a big white van. He hands me a balsa-wood tray brimming with fragrant strawberries. They look divine, very Wimbledon.

"From my mum, for Doamna Angela. And you."

"Wow, thanks, Filip, so kind. You were saying, about the timber?"

"We must measure your yard first."

"But we sent you the dimensions already, I think?"

"Yes, you did." Filip's smile could be described as imperious, perhaps because he knows his stuff and I don't. Oh well, let's just hope he prioritises our new fence, because there's only one thing worse than a tied-up dog, and that's two tied-up dogs. Especially if they're mine.

Luckily for them, Filip is soon striding around our yard, clutching a chunky steel tape measure, the sort that winds in, out, and all over the place. He has a studious air and lots of numbers to mutter. He scribbles in a notebook and shows his father, who lights another ciggie. Filip doesn't show his notebook to me; presumably such matters are beyond my comprehension. My job is to hold the end of a length of twine, while Silent Romeo walks backwards and unravels the rest of it.

"No, Mike," says Filip, "stay at ground level."

"Sorry."

I don't know why we are doing this and nobody bothers to explain. *Should I ask?* Probably not, I might sound overbearing, not to mention dim. Their expertise takes years to acquire, tricks of the trade and all that. I'll just watch and learn. I glance towards the house and spot Angela at a window. She raises a thumb. *Well done, guys.* Filip finishes his calculations, his dad disputes them, and they drive away to buy some wood.

A few hours later, Filip reverses the van, its canvas flapping, into our yard. We unload pine planks and six-foot posts, which smell like one of those little cardboard trees that people hang in their car because it smells like these.

Our neighbour Martin comes ambling down the lane, destination cow shed. Perhaps he'll bring us some fresh milk later. It's one of the nice things about living here. Unless you're his cow and wondering where your calf went.

"You're making a new fence," says Martin, with a grin. A friendly man of few words – most of which state the obvious – he seems tipsy today, but he's not our first wobbly neighbour and won't be the last. His gold teeth fascinate me – a full set of eighteen-carat choppers; when he smiles it's like someone opened the door of Tutankhamun's tomb. "But so much timber, Domnul Mike?"

"Yes, Domnul Martin, to stop our dogs escaping."

"It will stop your dogs escaping, but–" He's momentarily lost for words. Perhaps he thinks that our dogs ought to be tied up 24/7. If so, most of our neighbours would probably agree, but I don't.

"What are you thinking, Martin?"

"The wind. In a storm. That's what I mean."

"How do you mean – *that's what I mean?*"

"You may have problems, that's all. Bye." He wanders away, in his old wellies. His pants are baggy and his jumper looks likes he slept in it. I've seen his fence too – pretty rickety, as I recall.

Filip comes to ask me about Martin. When I mention bad weather, Filip reassures me that our fence will cope, *no problem.* He cracks a joke in Romanian about Martin being drunk. I don't quite get it, but I do learn a new word, which Filip translates for me.

"*Băgăcios* means *busybody,* like your neighbour."

We watch Martin swaying down the lane towards his cow shed. *Is he a drunken busybody?* Not really, but Filip probably knows more about fences than Martin does, given his expertise in all things construction. It's quite reassuring. And time to get back to work.

Tearing up and knocking down our old fence is the easy part, even under a scorching sun. We slam sledgehammers into warped grey planks and send them splintering. We push and pull at ancient posts – left and right, back and forth – until we prise them from their holes where glistening worms coil in confusion. It takes two hours, and when we're done, the old fence is strewn on the ground as if a hurricane hit our hill. We stash the timber at the back of the house, for winter fuel.

Now it's time to start the real work. First, we dig fifty-six bucket-sized holes, half a metre deep, in the unforgiving, pebble-filled terrain. *What are pebbles doing at 1000m above sea level?* No idea. I just wish they weren't here because it's bloody hard going. Mundane, mind-numbing toil, in fact. This is how it must have felt digging up the prairies of North America, to lay railroad tracks. Still, at least we have no hostile Apaches watching from the ridge. Just a lone hawk soaring in high circles; imagine being a mouse, looking up and seeing that thing swooping down at you, all talons and pointy beak?

"Mike."

"Yes, Filip?"

"Dig, if you want a fence."

"I'm digging."

Four hours later, we're done and duggered. Fifty-six holes, deep and round. Our yard looks like a course for rookie golfers.

Next, we daub treacly black bitumen on the bottom ends of fifty-six pine posts and lay them out, like giant matchsticks, to dry in the afternoon sun. Martin ambles by, carrying a pail of creamy milk. His eyes pop when he clocks our wooden posts with shiny black tips. He stands in the lane, talking to himself. He's been at the hooch again, probably.

Filip walks past me with his tape measure, and mutters, "Some real idiots around here."

Martin's golden grin suggests that he is thinking the same about us.

Next day, Romeo mixes quick-dry cement inside a rolling drum. A dozen sheep pause in the lane, apparently intrigued. Perhaps they want to learn how; perhaps they like all this grinding and clanking. Our dogs snap and snarl, lunging on chains. The sheep scuttle off, bolder and wiser.

We put the pine posts in their holes, one by one, and Romeo pours in the pale grey goo. Domnul Ionică nudges each post and Filip rests a spirit level on top. Our fence is coming along. So is Martin, except this afternoon he looks sober. Well, soberish.

Filip nudges my arm. "Domnul Băgăcios is back, lucky us."

Martin enters our yard, carrying a pail of milk that gleams in the sun. Angela comes out of the house, in T-shirt and shorts. She takes the pail. "Mulțumesc, Martin. Wait while I empty it?"

He waits, hands in his pockets, surveying the fruits of our labour. He peeps into a hole and says, "Concrete plugs?" He stands behind a post, cocking his head. "Certainly straight, I suppose."

"Strong, too." Filip chuckles, lighting a cigarette. "Still worried about the wind?"

"Of course," says Martin, caressing a wooden post.

"Well, if I were you, I wouldn't worry." Filip puffs grey smoke at the clear blue sky.

"Does your fence ever blow down, Martin?" I ask

"Not often, Domnul Mike, and anyway, it's easy to fix, isn't it?"

That's a good question, considering I've never fixed a fence. Jumped a few and sat on plenty, but *fix* one? Not me. Let's hope I never need to.

Angela reappears and gives the empty pail to Martin, along with a pack of good coffee, our favourite. He seems happy enough with today's exchange rate. "Mulțumesc, Doamna Angela."

Then he's off home, to his wife, across the valley. Milk from their cows is clean and of high quality. Angela will probably make a tasty rice pudding, as our workers have earned a treat, albeit not Martin's respect, I fear.

For the next few days, while the cement plugs set, Domnul Ionică & Sons turn their attention to other jobs. My help is not required, so I stay at my desk and catch up on some work. But every half hour or so, I gaze through my window to admire the wooden posts. *Such beauties!* Soon, it will be time to nail up the cross bars. Then we'll apply creosote, *and let slip the dogs of war.* Shakespeare said that. I wonder if the Bard duggeth holes for his fences?

I'm soon outdoors again, wearing overalls and a floppy sunhat, to creosote the posts and crossbars. It's a long job because it's a long fence – one hundred and fifty metres in all, not to mention seven bars high. But I'm enjoying the work, at least until Filip turns up. He saunters down the slope, shaking his head at me. "No, Mike."

"Had a feeling you might say that, what's up?"

Filip points. "This is not how we creosote a fence. Drip marks, see? You're doing it all wrong."

"Actually, I didn't paint that bit."

"So who did?"

"The little boy who lives down the lane."

"Is this a joke?"

"No, young Dragoş painted that bit. He was hanging around, asking questions. I think he wanted to have a go. So, I let him have a go."

"You let some village kid creosote the new fence?"

"His bike's bust and he's bored, or so he said."

"Not our problem. Don't let kids creosote the fence."

"I'll re-do his bits later. But for now, I'll just–"

"Mike, your brush, please? Give it to me."

Filip takes my brush, dips it in the drum of creosote and applies careful strokes to the wood. He pauses to admire his handiwork. "That's how, see?"

"Yes, Filip, but as I said—"

"OK, your turn. You'll need more creosote on the brush. Not too much, mind."

Filip hands me the brush and folds his arms. I crouch, and dip it into the pot, stirring gently. *Where are we going, with this?* In circles, I think. "Thanks, Filip. What are you working on?"

"I'm going to stay and watch you. To make sure you do it right, because creosote is rather expensive."

I can't believe my sunburned ears. I stare into the pot of shiny brown goop. Should I tell him I was painting ranch fences in Colorado when he was shitting in his nappies? Should I tell him to get back to work, because his time is my money? Should I tell him he's a busybody, rather *băgăcios,* actually? No, none of the above, because a bad vibe will prevail and the last thing we need is a belligerent builder – who knows what he might do, or not do? So, I apply caution, and creosote, and Filip monitors me until he's satisfied. Then he walks away. Just as well, lest I paint his nose.

Our builders depart for Bucharest a few weeks later, jobs done, leaving Angela and me to enjoy our renovated home and the rest of the summer. We've got new doors, a mezzanine, and an extension with big windows offering breathtaking views of Piatra Craiului, the twenty-six-kilometre mountain ridge. We've also got refurbished bathrooms, central heating, and a dog-proof fence. After twenty years of global travel and living in some dodgy dumps, it's nice to have a home at last.

Every morning, we lie in bed listening to house martins flutter in and out of their cup-shaped nests under our eaves. The big nest just above our bedroom window is a wonder to behold. How did they make it? The birds love to gossip too, perhaps about our home: *How did they make it?*

During the long sunny days, we toil in our vegetable patch, assisted sometimes by Doamna Dorina from up the hill, who's happy to share her expertise for a glass of gin and tonic in return.

Each evening, on the terrace, we watch swifts zoom and scream over our heads, in tight little flocks, as they hunt flying insects. After dark, I tilt back my wicker chair and gaze up, tracking satellites. The silver dots sail across the inky sky. I find it humbling to watch such marvels of the modern age, especially as it takes me half an hour to wire a plug.

Best of all, our two dogs are free to trot around our yard and bark the odds at any puss who passes: *Stay out, or we'll gobble you up.*

Our first autumn in the mountains is mercifully mild, but winter arrives with a rumble of grey clouds and driving sleet that lasts for weeks. The night before Christmas Eve, a merciless wind whips around our new home, whose isolated location seems the perfect target for a perfect storm, and, judging by the roar of the gale, we'll soon be in one. Sure enough, when the roaring, flashing, booming deluge hits us, our little house seems to wobble, as if about to take off like Dorothy's place in *The Wizard of Oz*. We huddle at a window, wide-eyed. Rain lashes down and the gods bawl their wrath. It feels almost personal, as if we have upset them by daring to settle on someone's sacred hill between two mountain ranges.

Groggy-faced and grumpy from lack of sleep, we're rather relieved to find ourselves still on planet Earth next morning. It's calm and sunny, imagine that. It's also Christmas Eve, and I wonder what little gifts Santa might bring us? Luckily, not much snow, just an inch, overnight. That's the first thing I notice, yawning behind the bedroom window. I open it and lean out, for some fresh air.

The second thing I notice is that one of the dog kennels has been blown twenty metres across the yard, upside down. Considering the kennel weighs about one hundred kilos, that was some gale.

The third thing I notice, at the back of the yard, makes me gawp in disbelief: fifty metres of our new fence is flat in the snow. The wind has uprooted six or seven of the wooden posts. They lie in a neat line, still attached to their concrete plugs, and resemble giant lollipops. Several of the fence's cross sections have been torn and scattered. Some of them appear to have been squashed by a marauding steamroller. Others hang askew from their posts, split into dark shards. We're not in Kansas any more. I curse under my breath and Angela joins me at the window.

"Wow," she says. "Where are the dogs, Mike?"

I'm dressed, downstairs, and out of the house in less than a minute, calling them. *What if they escaped over the bust fence to chase after sheep?* They'll kill some and there'll be hell to pay.

Our two dogs reappear soon enough and they seem calm and happy, not wild-eyed or blood-crazed. It could've been worse. *Thanks, Santa.* I chain them to their iron hoops, just like old times.

"Sorry, ladies, only until I mend our fence."

Then again, how? Buggered if I know. Should I phone Domnul Ionică, seeing as he built it? Perhaps I'll call his eldest son Filip and ask if he can drive up from Bucharest. I can guess his answer: *No, Mike.* Fair enough, but so much for our experts from the big city. It's too far away and so are they. What an unholy mess. I'd better ask a local. On Christmas Eve? *Great!*

I sit on a stranded post. It rocks beneath me like a seesaw. I look around at the stunning view. Those snow-capped mountains seem bigger than usual somehow, perhaps because I feel so tiny, insignificant, stupid, beaten by nature, put in my place. Perhaps I was too proud of our new fence? Hubris, you could say. This is payback. Nemesis? *Thanks again, Santa, just what I always wanted.*

Trudging back to the house, I spot a familiar figure in the lane: our neighbour Martin is on his daily trip to the cow shed. I walk to the front fence. That section is still erect, at least.

"Hello, Martin, any storm damage at your place?"

"Well, all that thunder scared my dogs, but otherwise no. Any problems up this end?"

"Plenty, look over there. Our fence blew down, all along the back." I point and he looks.

"Oh, your fence blew down, Domnul Mike. I did warn you."

"I remember. But how did you know?"

Martin shrugs. "Seven bars is too much wood. Also, you used concrete plugs, bad idea. A storm likes resistance, you provoked a battle you couldn't win."

"Very poetic, Martin, but Domnul Ionică and his sons told me this would be a strong fence."

"They're from Bucharest. They don't know how it is, up here. Perhaps in Bucharest, this fence would be a good fence, but not here. Look around, see the difference?"

Martin points left and right. Snow-dusted fields stretch towards the misty mountains. I see fences that are basic, battered, and ready to be recycled as firewood. I see that they probably cost a fraction of ours. But most of all, I see that they're still standing despite the horrendous storm. *How come?* We should've asked the locals before we built ours. It's a bit late for that, but here goes.

"So, tell me, Martin, how do I build a fence?"

"You mean fix this one, so she'll stay up?"

"I suppose so, yes."

He grins, delighted at my predicament or happy to help. Perhaps both. Either way, I have a feeling that Martin has waited too long for me to ask. His teeth sparkle in the sun. He looks like he ate gold bullion for breakfast, whereas I'll be munching humble pie, all winter, once this story gets out.

Oh, What Fun

Our first New Year in these glorious mountains. Tonight's the night, although a bitter wind is howling around our cosy home, the temperature has plummeted to minus 15°C, and snow lies knee-deep in the narrow lane outside. All things considered, we should probably stay here and pop a few corks, just the two of us. But, instead, at 8 p.m., we pull on woolly sweaters, salopettes, heavy boots, warm coats, hats, scarves, and thermal mittens. We grab our hiking poles, force open the front door, and strike out for the centre of the village. Because that's where the action will be.

It's hard going, though. Heads down, we thrust our poles left and right, inching our way, up hill and down dale. Snow sucks at our feet and the relentless wind seems bent on our submission. I feel as if we're off to explore the Antarctic. At our current rate, we'll reach our humble destination in about forty minutes. On the other pole, perhaps we won't reach it all. Angela taps my arm.

"Mike, we must be mad!"

The wind snatches my reply. Angela cups an ear. *What?* I point with my hiking pole. *Car coming, behind you.*

Bright beams from headlights flood the lane. Fir trees alongside glimmer in the glow, laden with snow. We seem to be trekking through a giant Christmas card. As the car trundles past, blurry faces stare from steamy windows. The driver beeps twice. Perhaps it means, *See you at the ball!* Perhaps it means, *Are you bonkers?* We wave mittened hands, plant our poles, and press on. Scott or what.

A huge horse trots out of swirling snowflakes with the customary red rosette on its bridle for protection against the evil eye. The horse is tugging a wooden sled. A familiar figure – our neighbour Liviu – sits upfront holding the reins. He nods *hello* as the sled purrs past us. A middle-aged man and woman huddle behind him. They're wearing matching jackets with fur-trimmed hoods. A thick woollen blanket is draped over their knees. *Tourists, probably.*

"That's the way to travel," Angela says, and we trudge on.

We arrive at the village hall around 9 p.m. Traditional *muzică populară* pumps from inside at deafening volume: high-pitched saxophone, bouncing bass, and a male vocalist with a keening voice. He sounds a bit sad. A lot sad, in fact, because his *pretty little chicken* has run off. Or so he sings, over and over.

We tread carefully up ice-encrusted steps and through a knot of chatting teenagers. The lads wear the traditional village uniform of short black leather jacket, skinny stonewashed jeans, and white hi-top trainers. The girls wear skimpy dresses, high heels, and lots of make-up. All of these youngsters seem happy to hang around outside the hall, shooting the breeze as if on summer vacation. Born and raised here, they're probably accustomed to freezing weather and have experienced far worse, no doubt.

Their happy banter subsides as we shuffle towards the entrance, dusted with snow like a pair of Inuit hunters just back from the frozen wilderness. Someone giggles, but not me. I have lockjaw, and a stalactite of snot hanging from my Rudolphian nose.

We edge into the tiny lobby, squeezing through a throng of adults, all busy buying bottles of beer and beakers of mulled wine from a trestle table. Clients at the back reach over the shoulders of those in front, to pay for drinks, some of which get spilled in the crush. But the mood is friendly and apologies come swift and sincere. Luckily, none of the men are *lookin' for friggin' trouble, pal,* so we slip unscathed between double doors and into the hall.

It's about the size of a tennis court, with a high ceiling, neon strip lights, and pristine white walls. The seats around the edge appear to have been purloined from a cinema or theatre – welded together in banks of five and upholstered in dark green velour, with wooden arm rests.

I was expecting to find a heaving crowd of a hundred at least. Instead, twenty or so bored-looking villagers sit watching two kids hop around the tiled floor. The little girl wears a silky red ballgown, black patent leather court shoes, and red lipstick. Her tiny partner wears a white shirt, black bow tie, and dark pants. Judging by their gooey grins, these two are very much in love or might be, one fine day. Grown-ups exchange proud smiles from the sidelines, as if plotting a marriage of convenience. *There's all that land, after all.*

On the stage at the far end of the hall, a DJ stands hunched over a mixing desk between large speakers. He grabs the microphone and announces a new song, which sounds like the previous one.

Angela spots some empty seats and we walk towards them, unzipping our coats. Several villagers greet us as we pass, but most just stare. An elderly woman nudges her neighbour and nods in our direction. We slump into stiff-backed velour seats and I try to look glad to be here. But the hall feels cold, looks bare, and is about as enticing as a waiting room in Siberia on a Wednesday afternoon.

"Still early," says Angela, reading my thoughts.

"Yup, perhaps it'll liven up later. Let's hope so."

"Here comes someone we know."

Our brawny neighbour waddles towards us. The last time I met Radu, he was wearing a bloodstained pinafore and slaughtering a calf. Tonight, he's looking somewhat dapper in a dark suit, white shirt, shiny purple tie, and a little black hat.

"Doamna Angela! Domnul Mike! *Servus!*"

We shake hands and I reply in kind, with the traditional greeting of so many Transylvanians. I like how it sounds but always feel as if I'm being bossy with a dopey waiter.

"*Servus*, Radu."

He beams. "You walked. I passed you in our car. Is yours bust?"

"No, car's fine. We walked because we don't drink and drive."

"Serious? Ach, don't worry, Mike, you're among friends."

I glance at the doleful faces watching us. *Certainly looks like it.*

Radu elbows me in the arm. "Anyway, drinks, let's get you some!" He leads me back to the lobby, while Angela stays to mind our stuff and chat with a bored-looking granny in a black headscarf.

When Radu and I return with mulled wine, three men in drab sweaters and jeans are onstage setting up for a concert. The youngest fellow plugs in a black cable, with the troubled look of one of life's roadies. The po-faced pensioner sits wincing at his keyboard as he plonks a single note, again and again. The third fellow, in his late twenties, stands adjusting the strap of his saxophone. He slips it over his head and nods half-heartedly at the DJ: *Ready.* The DJ fades down the music, the little kids pause mid-step on the floor, and all heads turn towards the stage.

We watch and wait, sipping our mulled wine. It tastes of sugar and spice, all things nice, and is deliciously warming – perfect after that icy trek. But I can't help wondering about these musicians with their bored expressions and tatty clothes. The baggy-eyed codger on keyboards seems ready for the knacker's yard. I edge closer to Radu and ask, "Are these guys any good?"

"Excellent," says Radu, with a gap-toothed grin. "Best for miles, just you wait."

Electronic drums boom, the keyboardist plays pretty chords, and the saxophonist adds a flurry of high-pitched notes. A dozen people rise to their feet and form a circle on the dance floor, arms up and holding hands. Radu joins them, squeezing in beside his wife Raluca. She's wearing a baggy white linen blouse, black skirt, embroidered waistcoat, and a bonnet. She spots Angela and beckons us. We raise our beakers of wine – *Cheers* – but prefer to watch, at least for now. Some of these dances can get tricky, you need to be nimble on your feet, and ours are still thawing out.

Within half an hour, the hall is full. Villagers stand three deep along the walls, clapping and whistling. Little kids scuttle about playing hide and seek. Grinning grannies tap their walking sticks up and down to the beat, which is increasingly irresistible, even for newbies like us. So far, the dance steps look easy enough.

"What do you reckon?" says Angela.

"Ready when you are, Ginger Rogers."

We relinquish our seats and step into the fray. Radu whistles encouragement from the opposite side of the circle. We grasp sweaty hands, left and right, and copy our neighbours as best we can: two steps forward, one step back, break off, turn, join up… *or was it two steps back?* Whatever, this is fun once you get the hang of it and even more if you don't.

The elderly man to my left taps my arm. "Domnul, this tune is from Sibiu. My dear wife and I danced it at our wedding, bless her soul." He wipes his eyes with the sleeve of his corduroy jacket.

We hop and bop to the same tune for twenty minutes, then the musicians launch into another one exactly the same. The dancing this time, however, is different. The big circle dissolves into several smaller ones and we drape our arms left and right around our neighbours' shoulders. We step twice clockwise, then once anticlockwise, so the circle rotates slowly back to where we started. *I've done this before, at a party in '94.* I turn to the silver-haired lady on my right and ask, "Are we dancing the *hora*?"

"I am, but you're not," she says. "Look what my feet are doing." She casts her eyes downwards and so do I. Her dainty little feet are doing exactly the same as mine are doing. *Well, sort of.*

Rosy-cheeked and flushed with fun, Angela and I take a break on a couple of empty seats, watching occasional snowflakes drift across the windows. "Worth that walk. Great party, this," I say.

"Band is amazing, don't you think?" says Angela.

We sit and watch. The two musicians whizz through their high tempos and complicated changes, scarcely missing a beat. Radu was right, they're excellent and know how to keep people happy.

Another of our neighbours – the one known as Tango – is whirling around the dance floor, his white smock open to expose a hairless chest glistening with sweat. He wears heavy gold rings and holds one arm aloft, snapping his fingers. His laughing wife Tamara clings to his waist, her head back and dark hair cascading down. Her long skirt twirls in the air and her shiny shoes tap a tattoo on the tiles. Truly, this couple is the life and soul of the party and everyone stands back, whooping encouragement, to give them more space to reel and romp. I feel like an extra in an opera and the lyrics of *La Habanera* spring to mind:

L'amour est un oiseau rebelle
Que nul ne peut apprivoiser!
L'amour est enfant de bohème
Il n'a jamais, jamais, connu de loi!

Angela catches my eye. "Where are you?"

"Miles away."

"I can see that. What are you muttering?"

"Love is a rebellious bird, that no one can tame. Love is a gypsy child; he has never, ever, known the law."

"Very romantic. It's probably the mulled wine."

"Actually, it's a song."

"Nice, did you make it up?"

"No, Bizet did. It's from *Carmen*. You liked the melody, remember?"

"Ah, yes." Angela fans her face with her hand. I wish I had a proper one for her, something Spanish with frilly edges. She'd make a good *Carmen*, with her dark eyes and brooding good looks. She wrinkles her nose. "Too much smoke, Mike."

She's right. The air is stale and stinky, but not a single window is open because if it were, here in Romania, everyone would die next day of pneumonia. "Time out?" I suggest, and Angela nods.

We make our way to the door, squirm through the busy lobby beyond, and stand on the icy steps. Three young lads stand nearby clutching smartphones and the glow illuminates their faces. One of them elbows the next fellow. "Text her, Mihai! Just text her, right now, and apologise!"

Mihai pockets his phone. His two friends shake their heads and roll their eyes. *Loser.*

Below us, the snow-covered road curls like a silver snake through the village. The wind has dropped and the thick grey clouds are drifting apart to reveal countless stars scattered across a black sky. It's heaven, out here. I stand beside Angela and point up. "Pole Star, see?"

"Which one?"

"That one. It's four hundred and thirty-three light years away, and four thousand times brighter than our sun. Or something."

"Certainly a beautiful night, now."

"Our walk home should be easier, at least."

"Actually, I've got a better idea." Angela pulls out her phone, thumbs a number, and gives me a wink. "Let's call Liviu."

"Liviu?"

"With the sled."

The horse-drawn sled arrives for us at 2 a.m. We make our excuses to Radu, Raluca, Tango, Tamara, and all the rest, and leave the party, clammy with sweat. The freezing air bites hard.

Our driver is not Liviu but his friend Gheorghe, who doesn't explain why. Gheorghe just beams at us with his moon face and beckons us aboard the sled. He's wearing a woollen waistcoat, tracksuit pants, no hat, and no gloves. We climb in the back and huddle under a blanket to keep out the chill, like a pair of tourists. Our driver sips from a small bottle, clicks his teeth and we're off.

The hardworking horse canters along and the sled hisses on smooth snow. Gheorghe perches upright, gripping the reins and bellowing gibberish. He seems tipsy. Sloshed, in fact. So sloshed, he can hardly speak. He turns towards us with a lop-sided grin, as if recovering from a stroke. Angela and I exchange worried glances. If the horse doesn't slow down, we'll soon be on TV.

BREAKING NEWS

DRUNKEN TREE KILLS THREE

I lean forward and nudge our driver gently in the back.

"Domnul Gheorghe, could you slow down, please?"

Gheorghe raises a thumb, then whips the horse. *Perhaps he misunderstood?* Our creaking sled careens around a corner and Angela yelps in fright, as well she might because if we meet a car coming the other way, we'll meet our maker too.

We grasp the slatted wooden bench, hoping for the best. We could jump out, I suppose, and roll down a snowy slope to safety, but that only happens in action movies. Oddly enough, Gheorghe seems to think we're in one and races around every bend as though we're chasing baddies. Or perhaps they're chasing us.

I turn to my wide-eyed wife. "What happened to Liviu?'"

Angela peeps over the blanket. "Maybe he changed his mind."

"And sent this nutter, instead. Should we stop him and walk?"

"Too cold."

"So, what do we do?"

"Pray. Who's the saint for safe travels?"

"St Christopher, but he's probably at a party."

Luckily for us, the horse tires quickly on the inclines, plodding and panting. *Champion the Wonder Nag.* Up we go, nice and slow. But on the down slope, when we canter, we'd beat Santa. Ironic, really, considering that one reason we decided to move to these remote mountains was that we'd had enough of kamikaze traffic in big cities, such as Bucharest with its legions of loony taxi drivers. Yet here we are, slipping and sliding towards an uncertain future in the early hours of New Year's Day. At least we'll go out with a bang. A whinny, even.

Trees flash by, their branches sagging with snow. Do beasts watch from the dense forest, ready to feast on our mangled bodies? Maybe Angela is right – we should pray. But to whom, the patron saint of horses? No idea. On the bright side, there's always the stars and look how they shine for us, at this special hour.

We glide downhill and onto a long, straight slope where our pace slows to a gentle slog. We may survive, it seems, after all. I nudge Angela and sing, *"Jingle bells, jingle bells, jingle all the way! Oh, what fun it is to ride…* you know this one, Gheorghe?"

I pause for a response. None comes. Our driver is looking down at his reins. Having a private moment, perhaps. Reflecting on another year gone by. Or maybe he's just fed up with Formula Horse.

"Gheorghe, are you ок up there? Gheorghe?"

I nudge him in the back. No response. His woollen waistcoat is probably too thick. I poke him harder. He jolts upright.

"Yes, Domnul Mike?"

"Good morning. Did you fall asleep, Gheorghe?"

"Only for a moment. Bit tired, you see."

"You should be tucked up in bed, not working," says Angela.

"True, Doamna, but Liviu told me to fetch you."

"So, where's Liviu?"

"Probably in bed with you-know-who."

Angela and I exchange puzzled glances; we don't-know-who and we don't much care. All we want is to get home, sometime this year. Decent of the horse to stay awake, at least. It seems to know this road like the back of its hoof, thank our lucky stars.

Despite a few near misses with low-hanging branches and a close encounter with an owl that swoops all a-flutter from the forest, we reach home in two pieces and pay Gheorghe for his trouble. He seems somewhat confused by the transaction, and stares at the money in his palm, as if wondering how it got there.

"Take care, Gheorghe, try not to crash on the way back."

"Crash, Domnul Mike? Me? Never!"

He gives the horse a stinging swipe with his quirt and the sled slithers away. We watch him go, around the bend.

"That was a ride to remember," says Angela.

"Or even forget. I'm just glad we made it home."

"Let's hope Gheorghe does."

Two days later, while we're out walking the dogs, we spot Gheorghe striding towards us. He's wearing a combat jacket, bright orange salopettes, and muddy wellies. Head down, and thinking hard by the look of it, he thrusts his long walking stick into the snow and seems not to notice us at first. Perhaps he's still suffering from a hangover. I wouldn't be surprised, if so.

"Afternoon, Gheorghe, how you doing?"

"Fine, thanks, Domnul Mike." He glances up but doesn't look fine. A crimson gash glitters on his forehead, his lower lip is split and swollen, and his left eye resembles a fried egg. Poor Gheorghe looks as though he's been in the ring with Mike Tyson.

"Ouch, what happened to you?" says Angela.

Gheorghe shrugs. "That's how it is, Doamna Angela."

I step closer, inspecting the damage. "You've been in a fight?"

"Nu, Domnul. I was in my sled, New Year's Eve."

"Hmm. So were we. With you, actually."

Gheorghe tilts his battered face. "Did I bring you home?"

"Yes, you did, thanks. But then what happened?"

"Had a crash. Fell out. Bashed myself on a rock, see?"

"On a rock?" Angela winces. "You're lucky to be alive."

"By the grace of God, Doamna, that's how it is."

"Sorry you got hurt but you were a bit tipsy that night."

"Tipsy, Domnul Mike?" Gheorghe eyes me like Cyclops.

"Tipsy and tired," says Angela, "you fell asleep on the way."

"And that's why we told you to be careful, Gheorghe."

"Careful, Domnul Mike? I'm always careful! The problem was Liviu's stupid horse, that's who. Anyway, I'm late and my sheep need their feed, so good day to you both, and Happy New Year."

Gheorghe marches away, swinging his stick and muttering to himself, before I can ask whether the horse was sloshed as well.

Carollateral Damage

"I wonder what happened here?" says Angela.

We pause on our New Year's Day walk and gaze at our neighbour's white picket fence. It's smashed to bits and her cottage garden looks as though an angry bull has passed through.

Angela shakes her head. "What a mess, poor Doamna Jeni."

"Something to do with last night, I bet. Someone got drunk and crashed their car or cart."

I scan the snow for telltale signs but see only footprints. Lots. Our two dogs lunge towards the fence. They've found a maroon smudge on a post. *Sniff sniff, lick lick.* I step closer.

"Bloodstain, that is."

"Oh, yuk," says Angela.

We pull the leashes, dragging the dogs up the lane, but after a few metres they stop again – paws splayed in the snow – and refuse to budge. This time, they've found clothing scattered in the slush. Our sort-of-Rottweiler Linda paws at a traditional Romanian blouse of embroidered cheesecloth, while our sort-of-Husky Sam pokes her snout into a white lace skirt with a waistband of bright brocade. A black woollen pinafore hangs from rusty barbed wire, nearby. They are traditional Transylvanian garments, the sort worn at a folk festival, or on New Year's Eve.

"Must've been quite a party, last night."

"But why dump expensive clothes?" says Angela.

"These are expensive?"

"I'll say. Handmade. They take ages. Cost a fortune."

We look around, wondering. Not a soul in sight. Angela picks up the skirt and blouse, shakes off the excess snow, and folds them carefully into a plastic bag, the one she brought for litter.

"Rubbish can wait. Fetch me that pinafore?"

"Sure."

Easier said than fetched, however, because the barbed wire is reluctant to give up its prize, at first.

"Don't rip it," says Angela.

Walking on, we agree that this puzzle, like most puzzles in Culmea, will be solved by time and gossip. We hear our first version of the truth about an hour later, at the same spot, on our way home.

Two young kids – Doamna Jeni's daughter Simona and her cousin Grigore from across the lane – are crouched in the slush. Wearing bonnets and boots, they're flanked by hens looking for whatever hens look for. Simona pokes a chunk of broken fence into a little snowman, for an arm. Grigore adds the other arm. It's nice to see them playing together, especially since their respective families are bitter foes in a long-running feud exacerbated by the proximity of their homes: two brightly-painted cottages that face each other, just a few yards apart.

Come spring, of course, both cottages will be decked out with hanging baskets, and the fields beyond will host cute lambs and cows that moo. Tourists will be charmed by the idyllic scene, clicking away with big cameras and wittering on about *paradise*. But they don't know the half of it, and neither do I.

Judging by what we see before us, however, there's hope for the next generation. It's New Year's Day, after all. We squelch towards the kids. Grigore turns, rises, and trudges up to meet us. *Splish-splash.*

"Doamna Angela, the fence got broken, come!"

"Yes, Grigore, we know. Any idea what happened?"

"Big fight, last night." Grigore's blue eyes dominate his face and his cheeks are rosy. Cute as a Disney cartoon. He's clutching a snowball, packed hard.

"A fight between who?" I ask.

Grigore looks at Simona. It's her fence, after all.

"Well, you see," says Simona, "Liviu Moraru and Costi came to our house dressed as women, for New Year."

"Who's Costi?" says Angela.

"He's from Brașov. He's staying with the Moraru family. Costi has too many brothers and sisters. My mum says that's why he came. He's seventeen. He tells funny jokes."

"And he smokes," says Grigore.

"Liviu and this Costi had a fight?" I ask.

Simona shakes her head. "No, they were just singing carols, for money. They had a drum and one of those big whips for making noise at New Year."

"Like this." Grigore lashes the air, from left to right, with his hand: *whoosh-crack.*

Simona rolls her eyes. "Anyway, they were singing, and then…"

We wait. And wait. "Then what, Simona?" I say.

Simona shrugs. "Then my Grandpa came out to give them money and… there was a fight."

"Because he gave them money?" says Angela.

Simona is silent, inspecting her gloves.

I turn to her companion. "Do you know, Grigore?"

"Do I know what, Domnul Mike?"

"Why there was a fight?"

"I'm not supposed to say."

"Is it a secret?"

Grigore gives Simona a sheepish glance. She glares back. "Say what you like, Grigore, it's not even true."

The silence is becoming awkward, so we move on.

"Perhaps we'll never know. Bye, then," says Angela.

Grigore scoots after us and looks ready to burst with excitement. "Simona's grandpa was drunk and wouldn't give Liviu and Costi any money and he said *you get lost* and there was a fight and that's why." He pauses for breath.

"My grandpa wasn't drunk!" yells Simona.

Grigore shrugs. "My dad told me different."

"Because he's a busybody," says Simona.

"No, he isn't."

"A dog-damn busybody, my mum said, so there."

Angela steps between them. "Let's not argue?"

Simona jabs a finger. "Grigore started it, not me."

"Do we know who broke your nice fence?" I ask.

"Well, let's think," says Simona, "maybe Grigore's dad?"

Grigore caresses his snowball. "Better shut up."

"I shouldn't even be speaking to you." Simona marches off, tramping slush. Hens scatter left and right, *What the cluck*.

"Then the police came," says Grigore.

"I'm not surprised." Angela opens her plastic bag. "Any idea who left these nice clothes in the snow? Liviu and Costi, perhaps?"

Grigore admires his perfect snowball. "Don't know."

"We'll ask around. Thanks, Grigore. *La Mulți Ani*."

Inevitably, we hear the most interesting version of The Big Fight from our six-year-old neighbour Dragoș. If you want to know what's really going on in Culmea, just ask little Dragoș.

We're out in our yard, wearing salopettes and rolling snow into balls of various sizes. Our dogs run towards the fence, barking. Dragoș comes down the lane, wearing an oversized puffer jacket of red, green and white. Black mittens dangle on cord from his cuffs. He pauses to pat our dogs through the fence then gawps at us. "Domnul Mike, what you making?"

"Snow dogs."

"Snow dogs?"

"Like snowmen, but dogs. These will be ears, and paws, see? We'll add a bit of carrot later, for a nose."

Dragoș looks mystified. "I never made one of those."

"But you've made a snowman?"

"Two, last week, with Tata."

"Is he going back to Italy? Did he find a job?"

"Yes, in an abb.. an abbat… a place where they chop animals."

"Abattoir. Did Santa bring you anything nice?"

"Yeah, new phone. But my big sister has borrowed it. She gave me her old one, just for a while. Domnul Mike?"

"Yes?"

"Some policemen went to Simona's house."

"At New Year?" says Angela, brushing snow from her gloves.

Dragoș nods. "Because there was a fight, a big one."

"About what?"

"About drinks. And cake. And not getting any."

"Oh dear, we've been wondering what happened."

Dragoș places a foot on the lowest bar of the fence and hoists himself higher. "I know."

"You do?"

"Yup."

"Perhaps one day you'll tell us."

"I can tell you now if you like."

"ок, if you have time."

"Well, what happened was, Liviu and his friend Costi – who's a smoker, by the way – got dressed up as ladies. You couldn't even tell it was them. They took a drum and a whip and went about singing carols for drinks and cake. Or money, if you've got some. They came to our house and Tata gave them drinks. Everywhere they went, people were giving them drinks. And sometimes cake. But Simona's grandpa didn't give them anything, not even a bit of cake. So, they said bad words to him. Then, Simona's grandma came out and shouted at them, so Costi swung his whip at her. Then, she slapped his face and everyone started fighting, even Simona's Uncle Nichifor and he's handicapped. And during the fight, Costi kicked the fence in. You can still see it. Just walk down there and look. All bust."

"We saw it, and thanks for explaining," I say.

"Domnul Mike?"

"Yes?"

"I didn't finish."

"Sorry, go on."

"So then, Simona's Uncle Nichifor kicked Costi in the ribs. You could even hear them cracking."

"Uncle Nichifor with the bad legs?"

"Maybe he punched him instead. And Simona's grandpa held an axe to Costi's head and Costi shouted, *Liviu, run away or they'll kill you, too.* And that's when Liviu ran away."

"My goodness. Did Costi get killed?"

"No, he's too smart. He's a smoker, you see."

"How do you mean?"

"Well, when he was lying on the ground, waiting to be killed, he told them he was a smoker and needed a cigarette. So, they let him stand up. But his cigarette pack was actually an iPhone and that's how he called the police to come and save him."

"Ah, so that's why the police came?"

"Yes, and Simona's grandma gave them some coffee and cake, and the policemen said, *Give some to Costi too.*"

"Thanks, Dragoș. How do you know all this? Were you in the street at midnight? Or in Simona's house when the cops came?"

"Domnul Mike."

"Yes?"

Dragoș points through the fence. "You forgot to make ears for your snow dogs. Dogs have ears."

"We didn't finish them, yet."

"OK, *la revedere.*"

He waddles home through the slush. I watch him go and can't help wondering. The truth is out there somewhere, buried under an avalanche of rumours. As for Dragoș, he's quite a storyteller for his age and might make a good writer, one day. Or perhaps he'll end up in politics, flanked by acolytes hanging on his every fib. Either way, he's certainly got a knack for drama, motive, and detail. It's the little things that count, after all.

"Mike."

"Yes, Angela?"

"Make some ears."

The Enemy Within

Our beautiful cushion – my favourite – is not on the sofa, where it should be. It's not in my study, where it could be. And it's not in the attic, where it would never be. I know, because I've checked all those places. Our beautiful cushion is missing, disappeared, gone.

"Cushion, did you say?" Angela pokes at the keyboard of her laptop. Listening, but not really.

"The zebra hide cushion. From Namibia. It's vanished, Angela."

"Must be somewhere."

"It should be on the sofa. The gazelle cushion goes on the right, the zebra on the left."

"Since when?"

"Since whenever I tidy up. I arrange them like that. It's symmetrical. *Zebra, gazelle.* Looks nice. Well, it used to look nice. But now there's no zebra cushion, see?" I point at the sofa.

Angela glances across. "It'll turn up. When did you notice?"

"Fifteen minutes ago. I can't find it anywhere. This is weird."

"Did you check the garage?" Angela turns back to her laptop and continues checking something more important.

"The *garage?* Why would that cushion be in the garage, Angela?"

"You never know. Anyway, if you check, please bring me a bottle of mineral water?"

The cushion is not in the garage and our little jeep will not answer my questions, so obviously it knows something. I grab a bottle of mineral water from a shelf, carry it into the house and pour a glass for Angela, who says, "Well?"

I pace the room, checking corners and peeping under cupboards. "No luck. Know what I think?"

Angela sips water, calm in my crisis. "No idea."

"Someone stole it."

"Obviously."

"Someone who liked our cushion."

"Absolutely."

"Someone who's been in the house."

"Tell me you're not serious."

"I'm serious."

"Mike, don't be silly, who would do such a thing?"

"Someone who's been in the house. They saw it and they—"

"A visitor stole our zebra cushion? Don't be ridiculous."

"Angela, a cushion doesn't just vanish. It was on the sofa, there. Now it's gone. So, you tell me. What do you think?"

"Paranoia, is what I think. People don't steal cushions."

I stand near the big window, looking at the mountains capped with snow under a pale blue sky. Neat little farmhouses dot the valley below us. It's a glorious view and we're lucky to live here, which makes it all difficult to believe a friend or neighbour would steal from us. But someone did. Someone out there knows where our lovely cushion is. Someone who waited until our backs were turned. I'll crack this little mystery. I just need to think.

"I have an idea, Angela. I'm going to look at some photos."

"Photos?"

"Yes, for clues. Ovidiu and Alina visited in November, right? We sat on the sofa for a selfie. If the cushion was on the sofa, we'll be able to see it. That will provide a time frame."

"Unless one of us sat in front of the cushion."

"I hadn't thought of that."

"Who do you think you are, Lieutenant Colombo?"

"We all start somewhere. I'll start with photos."

Settled at my laptop, I browse folders of various snaps until I spot what I'm looking for.

"Angela, I found one, come and look. Here's our zebra cushion, on the sofa, in late November. Now it's early January. That means our cushion disappeared sometime in December, probably."

"Hmm, I see what you mean. It's all a bit weird, I must admit. But why would someone take it?"

"Because it was unusual. It was desirable. That's why we bought it, remember. I'd say it's one of the nicest things from all of our time in Africa. I loved that cushion. Really, I did."

"Yes, it's nice."

"Was nice."

I tap a thumbnail against my teeth, gazing at the photo. Ovidiu is one of my oldest friends. Wearing a big woolly hat, that day. The rest of us are grinning like idiots in our big sweaters. Tipsy, by the look of it, lounging left and right. My elbow is on the zebra cushion. Environmentally-friendly too, that cushion, as I recall.

"What are you thinking?" says Angela.

"When I was a news reporter, a policeman told me you need three things to commit a crime: the motive, the means, and the opportunity."

Angela folds her arms. "Go on, Lieutenant?"

"Let's think. Who's been here since this photo?"

"Mike, you can't just accuse one of our guests."

"I'm not accusing, it's just a question: who's been here? Someone with a bag, say, big enough to hide a cushion."

"You're nuts."

"Agreed, but that's irrelevant. Who's been here since late November? Doamna Dorina, for a start. She often drops in."

"And she's too nice to steal. From us or from anyone else."

"Exactly, so we rule her out. But who else? What about all the the kids who come for your English classes and my ukulele classes? They're here every week. Oh, and they bring bags."

"Which are too small. And they're nice kids. You can't accuse kids."

"I'm not accusing, I'm eliminating. Suspects."

"Suspects, now?"

"Candidates, possibilities, who cares? People who've been here. Your sister visited us just before Christmas, for example."

"It wasn't her."

"Fine, agreed. But who else has been here? Think. At least, try."

"I'm trying, but I don't like doing it."

"What about those guys who fixed our wood-burner?"

"That was after Ovidiu and Alina's visit."

"You're right. That's why Ovidiu wore a woolly hat, in this photo. He was cold because our wood burner was bust. And those guys who fixed it were in and out all day. It could've been them."

Angela shakes her head. "It wasn't them."

"Because?"

"They're Evangelical Christians. They built that little chapel in the village. They're decent folks. No alcohol, remember?"

She's right. I remember. *Three workmen and not a drop, all day.* It seemed unusual. Most workers up here drink something on the job, or afterwards. But those guys? Not even a beer. Hallelujah.

"Then again, Angela, just because someone doesn't drink, it doesn't mean they don't nick things. Hitler was a vegetarian."

"What?"

"Just saying." I gaze at my laptop screen. At the photo. At the zebra cushion. Under my elbow. Now you see it, now you don't. "There must be a way to find the culprit, Angela."

"There is a way."

"Like what?"

"The security cameras. Just wind back the tape and check the footage. On the monitor upstairs. If you're so determined."

"Great idea, why didn't I think of that?"

"Because you're not Colombo."

Talk about easier said than done. After an hour of staring at grainy footage from four cameras inside and outside the house, my eyes hurt and my enthusiasm is waning. Angela brings tea and sympathy. "Any luck?"

"Needle in a haystack. I've only checked two days of tape, so far, and that's from early December. This will take ages."

Angela looks at the monitor. "I can't even see the sofa."

"Because the internal cameras don't show it."

"Great. What about the external cameras, any clues?"

"Just neighbours walking up and down the lane. Watch."

I press a button and Angela chuckles, pointing at the monitor.

"There's what's-his-name, and here comes Linda to bark at him. And there's Sam with her bushy white tail."

"Great guard dogs, not. We need a Doberman."

"Forget it, Mike, it was just a cushion, a souvenir. And, actually, to be honest, we probably shouldn't have bought it."

"Because?"

"It's not nice to kill zebras."

"Agreed. But that particular zebra had died of natural causes. The lady in the shop told us. Our cushion was an eco-cushion, handmade by local women."

"Hmm, rings a bell. Good memory. Oh well, whoever took our eco-cushion must have liked it and now they're happy."

"I'm not."

"That's life, Lieutenant. Anyway, bedtime soon."

"So much for these expensive security cameras."

I press a button and the monitor screen fades to black, instantly. *Whatever happened to the little white dot in the middle?* Televisions use to fade to a little white dot when it was bed time. And I used to trust people. So much for friends and neighbours.

Nights slide into days and days slide into weeks. I no longer muse on our domestic mystery, except when tidying up, because that's when I remember. I place the gazelle cushion on the right side of the sofa, then stand back and look at the vast empty space on the left. Colombo would've cracked this nut, by now.

Come April, we busy ourselves with seasonal tasks – digging over the vegetable patch, planting bulbs in the flower beds, and fixing broken fences. It's hard work but must be done. Some chores are easier than others. My favourite is spring-cleaning the dogs' kennels.

I know it's time, because Linda and Sam drag their winter blankets from the kennels as if to say, *Too hot, don't need this in there.*

I do Linda's place first, at the back of the house, facing the jagged mountain ridge of Piatra Craiului. Linda comes to watch, strutting about with her tail up and tongue out, grinning her gratitude. She's house-proud, almost, and who wouldn't be? These are good strong kennels, well designed and made in Romania by a company that knows what good doggies need.

I pick up her musty blanket and fold it in two. "All done with this, eh Linda? I'll give it a wash before next winter."

Next, I lift the kennel's heavy roof and prop it open with a short log, then lean inside and use a stick to push Linda's bedding of dry grass out through the arched entrance. The grass has been squashed flat over winter and resists my efforts at first, but when it's all removed, I fetch a brush and sweep out the remaining dust. Next, I empty a big sack of new dry grass into the kennel and spread it evenly. Job done, I remove the log, lower the roof, and Linda slithers inside to check.

Sam's kennel is around the front of the house, facing the Bucegi mountains, and the same routine applies – I lift the heavy sloping roof, prop it open, lean inside, and shunt the squashed grass out through the arch. Except, this time my stick nudges against something in the corner of the kennel. Something black, square-ish, and about the size of … *surely not?*

I look closer, prodding with my stick. The dark square is firm but spongey, and it wrinkles when pressed. It appears to be made of black leather and has a little hand-sewn tag with red letters: *Made In Namibia.* I flip the object over and gawp.

The distinctive stripes are dusty after five months in the kennel, but, yes, this is zebra hide. Our missing cushion is perfectly intact, except for a semi-circle of small indentations in the leather backing, where someone has carried it, in her sharp teeth, from our house to this kennel. Sam or Linda? *The crafty buggers.* They tend to swap homes, so who knows. But one of them will, I bet.

Clutching the cushion, I extract my head from the kennel and march towards the yard. Linda trots around the corner of the house, tail wagging. I brandish the cushion. "Was this you?"

Linda tilts her head and seems baffled. *Huh?*

I cup a hand to my mouth and yell, "Sam, come here!"

She's fifty metres away, by the fence, watching cows in the field on the other side. I call louder and she bounds up the slope towards me, ears pricked. Expecting a treat, no doubt. She looks like a Husky, ready to drag your sled a thousand miles. Or nick your cushion and carry it twenty yards. I show her Exhibit A.

"Was this you?"

She stops and stares, legs splayed, then turns quickly and scoots away, tail between her legs, towards her favourite hiding place – a cool and dark recess under the wooden terrace. It's where she buries bones and hatches plans. She wants a place to hide, but I want answers.

I tramp towards the terrace and peer underneath. Sam is crouched on the rocky ledge, three metres back, where I cannot reach. She avoids eye contact, ears down, licking her lips and quivering with shame. *It's a fair cop.* I back off, wagging a finger.

"You bad girl. Bad girl."

Linda appears at my side, head dipped and her big, brown eyes glittering in the dark at Sam. *I told you they'd find out.*

Sitting on a tree stump, brushing dried grass from the zebra hide, I think about motive, means, and opportunity. The last two conditions are easy – our sly doggy had the means because her strong jaw could easily carry this cushion. As for opportunities, yes, our dogs are allowed indoors when a bad thunderstorm scares them to shuddering wrecks, and they do slip inside to raid the cats' food bowls, sometimes. But the former occasions are rare and the latter occasions are a case of *Get in, gobble up, and get out.*

If Sam's opportunities represent a puzzle, her motive remains a complete mystery, at least to me. For example, why steal a cushion unless you want to chew it? Why is this one still in perfect condition? Did she just like the vivid black and white stripes? Did she think they would look nice in her home? I'll never know and she'll never tell. But I know someone who might like an update.

I walk towards the vegetable patch, hiding the cushion behind my back. It's a lovely sunny day, but at times like this, what you really need is a grubby white raincoat and a half-smoked cigar.

Angela is planting beans. She looks up and rubs soil from her fingers. "Hi, Mike. Nearly finished here. How are the kennels?"

"Nearly done. There's just one more thing…"

English for Beginners

"Domnul Mike, can you teach my son English?"

Our neighbour has twinkly blue eyes and an optimistic smile, so I feel a bit guilty when I say, "Sorry, Raluca, but no, my Romanian isn't really good enough."

She leans forwards, dragging her seat closer to mine. Her pendulous breasts sway beneath her baggy T-shirt. She's bra-less, and her bemused expression says I'm clueless.

"Domnul Mike, my little Emil already knows how to speak Romanian. I want him to know English and I'll pay you."

"But Raluca, how would I explain the grammar? Teaching language, especially to youngsters, is a special skill."

"You speak Romanian when you teach ukulele, Emil tells me. You speak it in both classes. With older kids *and* youngsters."

I could tell her that's partly the problem: these days I get precious little time to myself. But that would sound selfish.

"Raluca, music is easier. I use diagrams and sound. I show them where to put their fingers. Language is all words. I'd need to speak English, which would be hard for Emil and not fair on you."

She sits back, arms folded. "Hmm."

Her gaze travels across the table and settles on her husband Radu. He shrugs and pours *țuică* into my glass. Perhaps he hopes it will help. He's right and wrong. We clink our drinks, *cheers,* and Radu turns towards the TV screen on their kitchen wall. It's so high up, you need a neck brace to watch it, but Radu just needs the weather forecast and here it comes.

A glamorous young presenter in a revealing dress predicts rain in Transylvania. Lots of it. Raluca shakes her head. *Tut-tut*. She looks increasingly fed up. Maybe it's that dress.

"Perhaps I could teach Emil?" says Angela.

"Yes!" Raluca raises her beefy arms in victory. One breast flops south east and the other slithers to the sunny south west.

Needless to say, word travels around the neighbourhood and five more children sign up for Doamna Angela's English classes, to be held at our home. Her teaching materials – exercise books, folders, marker pens, flip charts, and a sturdy whiteboard on tubular steel legs – arrive by courier. So far, so good, and on the eve of session one, our dining room resembles a classroom. Angela checks her inventory and I stand nearby, trying to be helpful.

"Ever done this before, Angela, teach English?"

My wife is too busy to reply but, as they say in Romanian, *Tăcerea e un răspuns*. Silence is an answer.

The cowbell above our front door jangles forty minutes before the class is due to start. I peep from a window and see six young kids – three girls, three boys – in the lane beyond our fence. Emil in the Real Madrid top yanks hard on the bell cord. The smallest girl – Adelina under that straw hat – is hopping about like a spring lamb. Bianca with the pigtails is chatting to handsome Remus, who's playing it cool, as ever, collar up and hair gelled; he's seven going on seventeen. Simona is crouched down and fiddling with her shoe, watched by little Dragoș who has one finger up his nose. *Turn left at the bridge,* as my mother used to say.

I open the gate and they bundle past me – *Bună ziua, Domnul Mike* – into the house. Simona trips in the rush and falls flat. Such are the perils of hosting a bunch of energetic kids.

They jostle for seats in our dining room. Five-year-old Adelina, cutest of the cute, runs a dainty finger along a crack in the mahogany table. She has blonde hair and a steady gaze.

"Your table is broken, Doamna Angela."

Angela shrugs. "Hope not, Adelina. Mike, could you pass me the box of marker pens please?"

"Sure. Want me to hang around, just in case?"

"Good idea." Angela surveys her pile of books and printed sheets. "OK everyone, time to start."

After a brief introduction, she asks her pupils how much English they know and where they've learned it. Seven-year-old Dragoș raises a hand. His oversize watch slides down his forearm and his mouth is a perfect pout. "Doamna Angela."

"Yes, Dragoș, you first."

"That magnet is upside down." He points at the fridge. Heads turn. Everyone looks at the fridge.

"He's right," says Bianca, pigtails swinging. She rises from her chair and points at our miniature *Mona Lisa*. "This one's upside down, Doamna Angela. Should I turn it the right way?"

Angela smiles. "Thank you, Bianca, please do."

"Like this?"

"Perfect, thank you. Now let's carry on."

Dragoș raises his hand again. "Doamna."

"Yes, Dragoș?"

"Who's that lady?"

"Which lady?"

"On your magnet."

"She's *The Mona Lisa*, a famous painting."

"She's who?"

"Never mind, Dragoș, can you answer the question?"

"The question?"

"About learning English, that's why we're here."

"Oh." Dragoș bows his head, lost for words.

Adelina sits up, all smiles. "I learn English from watching TV. We watch films and stuff. Me and my sister, that is."

"And MTV sometimes," says cool dude Remus. He's wearing cologne. I can smell it from here.

Emil nods, nibbling on a thumbnail. "We also learn English in school. But not much."

"OK," says Angela, "so, tell me something you've learned in school. One at a time, please."

The kids take turns explaining how a young priest teaches them English once a week using an app on his phone. Angela listens with interest. "The priest uses an app?"

Six little heads nod, and Bianca says, "He teaches us words about fruit. Last time, we did pine… pine-something, anyway."

"Pineapple," says Remus, with a yawn.

Angela uncaps a marker pen and invites the kids to write on the whiteboard any words they know from the fruit section. Nobody volunteers. *Tăcerea e un răspuns*.

Eventually, Emil slides from his chair, shuffles to the front of the class, and writes *APPELLE*, which might win him top marks for something, if this were a French class. Remus covers his brow with a hand and peeps through splayed fingers, in mock shock. Angela looks at the board, then at me.

"Doamna," says Adelina, gazing around at the paintings, the lamps, the sideboard, the mirror, the masks, the little sculptures, and the bookshelf. She looks puzzled, as though she's lost something rather important.

"Yes, Adelina, is everything OK?" says Angela.

"Your house is like a shop."

"A shop? How do you mean?"

"It's got lot of things in it."

The others nod. *A shop, definitely, we've been in shops.*

"I have an idea," says Angela, "please could you write in your new exercise books any words that you know in English. If you like, you can write things that we find in shops. Or you can write down the names of things in this room. Up to you."

"In our exercise books?"

"Yes, Bianca."

"On the first page?"

"Yes, Simona."

"Should we write the date as well?"

"If you like, Adelina."

"Doamna Angela."

"Yes, Dragoş?"

"Your tap keeps dripping." He points at the sink and everyone turns to look. Angela glances at me. *Hey, Janitor.*

The children hunch over their exercise books, scribbling away. Some seem to relish the task but others soon lose interest and slump in their seats, frowning; presumably studying English is harder here than with Father *Appelle* across the village. Adelina chews her pen and looks around, searching for inspiration, perhaps. She raises a hand. "Doamna Angela, you have no TV." She looks baffled. Perhaps she'd rather be at home, watching a film.

Angela joins me in Janitor's Corner and murmurs, "After I go through their vocabulary, we'll pause for refreshments, then finish with basic conversation. What do you reckon?"

"Sounds good, if they can stay awake."

Time is almost up, when Angela writes on the whiteboard:

WHO?
WHAT?
WHERE?
WHEN?
HOW?
WHY?

She caps her pen and says, "Let's practise conversation. I'd like each of you to say a question beginning with one of those useful words. There are six, see? That's one each, but choose whichever you prefer. Raise your hand when you're ready."

Simona waves at us. *"How do you do?"*

"Excellent, Simona, well done."

"When is Christmas?" says Emil.

"Good," says Angela, "I'll write these on the board."

Bianca raises a hand. "Doamna! *Where is the cow?"*

"Why is Real Madrid very good?" says Remus.

"Yes, well done. Dragoș, perhaps you could try next?"

Dragoș puts his head down. *Perhaps not.* Little Adelina is admiring the view in our big mirror. *Perhaps I'll work in a shop.*

"Doamna."

"Yes, Simona?"

"Under this table, there is a red cat rubbing on my leg."

Everyone looks under the table, where our ginger cat is walking in tight circles with his huge fluffy tail sticking up.

"Don't worry, says Angela, "Roy won't scratch you."

"We've got a cat," says Dragoș, "but Grandma kicks it out."

"Dragoș?"

"Yes, Doamna?"

"Can you make a question from one of these useful words?"

Dragoș pouts at the whiteboard. *"How do you do?"*

"Well, yes," says Angela, "but that was Simona's answer. Can you try to think of a new one, perhaps?"

Dragoș looks ready to weep. Angela writes his answer up.

"Don't worry, Dragoș, that was fine. Now, Adelina, could you finish off for us, please?"

Adelina turns from the mirror. *Who, me?*

Angela points at the list. Adelina grimaces and exposes her lower teeth. She resembles a chimp hoping for a banana. The other kids watch and wait. Remus drums fingers on the table. Emil inspects a crack in the mahogany.

"Well?" says Angela, "any ideas, Adelina?"

Adelina sighs, caressing her blond curls and staring at the board. Her eyes are ice-blue but darker around the edge. She's a picture of innocence – a sweet little village girl who probably idles away summer afternoons cradling kittens in a hayloft.

"Doamna Angela, do I have to say something new?"

"It would be more helpful if you could, Adelina, yes."

Adelina wrinkles her button nose. Angela folds her arms and looks a bit weary. Teaching is hard work.

"Well, Adelina? How about something you remember from a book? Or even from a film, if you prefer. Does that make it any easier?"

"Yes, now I've got one." Adelina seems relieved, all smiles. *"What the fuck."*

Titus & Iacob

"Look at that. Just what we need, I reckon." I point into our neighbour's yard, as we walk by.

"A pig?" says Angela.

"No, under the woodpile, see?"

"I see a cat, and we've got five."

"I mean the platform thing, under the logs."

We stop and peer through the fence, at a neat stack of wood that measures about three metres high, three metres wide, and ten metres long. It looks like a single-decker bus made of logs, and sits on a simple but sturdy wooden platform raised some twenty centimetres off the ground for air to circulate underneath.

"What do you reckon, a platform like that, under our logs?"

"Good and strong, yes," says Angela, "it would do the job."

"Look how the design keeps the logs secure. Clever, eh?"

"Very."

At each end of the pile, a wooden barrier is propped up by two silver birch trunks that slope away at an angle of forty-five degrees. As far as I can see, the bottom ends of the trunks have been shaved and probably sharpened to points that rest securely in the ground, out of sight. The logs – five hundred or so – sit in tight layers on the platform between the barriers, ready for the wood-burner, come winter. A thick plastic sheet sits on the top layer and is tied down with cord, to keep rain off. Talk about convenient.

"Let's call Titus and ask who made it." I pull out my phone.

"Probably Titus," says Angela.

Titus drives his big black horse and long wooden cart into our yard next day at 8 a.m., as agreed. Our dogs prance in circles, yipping threats at the horse. A red rosette – traditional protection against the evil eye – is attached to its bridle. As for the marauding hounds, the horse just blinks at them: *Neigh problem*.

Half a dozen tree trunks lie in the cart. Young trees, by the look of it – their bark is smooth and pale green not brown and knobbly.

Titus hops down from his seat. He's a small, wiry fellow in his mid-thirties, dark-eyed and curly haired. Friendly enough but doesn't say much and, like so many locals available for a fee, he'll work quickly and with minimal fuss because he's keen to get back to his cows, sheep, you name it. Last winter, Titus fixed our cracked water pump, crouching for an hour in our concrete pit, minus 20°C. You want a job done, call Titus. He's worked abroad, too, and knows what's what. In his free time, he plays footy with the local lads. Likes to win, so I hear. He also likes to beat people up, despite his diminutive stature. Attacked a neighbour, with a stick, in the dark, some say. We have no idea why and we don't much care. We just need a sturdy platform so we can stack our wood near our burner for when winter hits. Titus is the man.

Our higgledy-piggledy pyramid of sawn logs sits four or five metres high and twenty metres around the base, by rock of eye.

Titus stands rubbing his bristly chin. "Lots of wood, Domnul Mike."

"For the next two winters, we hope."

"You need two separate platforms for this lot. Lucky I brought enough poles. Better safe than sorry. You said you've got some scrap, for the base?"

I lead Titus across the yard and point to our pile of discarded planks, beams, and bits of old gate. "Can you use that?"

"Yeah, plenty."

Angela joins us from the veg patch, wearing green wellies and gardening gloves. "Hi Titus, got everything you need?"

"Yes thanks, Doamna Angela, except a radio."

"A radio?"

"For some music, while I'm working."

I raise a thumb. "No problem, there's one in the shed. Wait."

My little Sony shortwave is twenty-five years young and spattered in paint, just like the one my dad owned in garden sheds gone by. Hardly surprising really, since, as Oscar Wilde said, *All men turn into their fathers, which is their comedy. They don't turn into their mothers, which is their tragedy.* Or something.

I bring the radio to Titus. He inspects it and says, "Quite old."

I have a feeling he means, *Quite crappy,* in which case, I should probably mention its sentimental value.

"Bought that for my first trip to Romania in 1994. Still works."

"Uh-huh." Titus selects a channel, cranks up the volume, and the hills are alive with diddly-diddly, otherwise known as *muzică populară*. I'd forgotten – Titus loves this stuff and plays it all day, in his pink cottage, one hundred metres from here. You'll often hear it when you walk by.

Titus beams. "You like this music, Domnul?"

"Very nice."

"Now we can start. Can you help me lift the poles out?"

"No problem."

Yes, problem. We lift the first trunk from the cart, hauling an end each. *Jesus H. Redwood, it weighs a fucking ton.* I've got two plasticine arms and five more of these big buggers to go.

Titus grins, hoisting his end. "OK, Domnul Mike?"

I grin back. The horse blinks. *Neigh problem.* We toss the trunk and let it roll. Soon, all six lie side by side and my biceps are aquiver. "Sure you can manage this job alone, Titus?"

"No problem."

"Good. I mean, I'd help more, but I've got a deadline."

"If I need help, I'll just call Iacob."

"Ah, Iacob, yes." *Iacob the cross-eyed, forty percent alcohol, half-brother?* This should be fun.

I wash my hands, check for splinters, and return to my desk to check for typos. Mistakes in *spellign*, that sort of *thnig*. Editing requires a lot of concentration because mistakes are like flies in a summer kitchen – zap one and two more appear. Someone should invent Typo Spray. *Directions for Use: Aim the aerosol at your laptop screen and press the button. Watch the bgugres die.*

Titus is soon hammering and sawing, and music from my old radio drifts up loud and diddly from the yard. Summer's here.

"Mike, take a break, come and see our platform." Angela peeps through my doorway, beckoning me. "Iacob is here, too."

"Sober?"

"Hope so."

I walk out to our terrace and peep over the rail into the yard below. *Wow, nice.* Titus and Iacob have almost finished the first platform: two robust wooden barriers face each other, ten metres apart, like hoardings for rival advertisements. Each barrier is supported by four tree trunks – two are vertical and two slope into the ground. Iacob is placing the last of a dozen planks on the rough grass between the barriers, equidistant like railway sleepers. Titus crouches to shove chunks of wood under each plank to raise it off the grass, nice and level with the ones behind him, like a boardwalk. The Drifters would approve: *Boardwalk, boaaardwalk.*

So far, so good. Our helpers should be finished in a few hours, if the weather holds. One more platform to do. Then we'll stack our winter fuel on top and say *La revedere* to our jumbled pyramid of logs. I check the sky for grey clouds but see only white, fluffy ones. Some have ears and resemble giant Angora rabbits.

"*Bună ziua,* Domnul Mike!" Iacob calls up from the yard. He's holding a wooden stake for Titus to whack. Titus raises a sledgehammer and swings it down, hard. THUNK! Iacob howls, sucks his thumb, then grins at me.

Just kidding. He seems in a jovial mood, full of fun and possibly hooch.

We serve them lunch on our terrace: cheese pie, tomato and olive salad, bread, glasses of sparkling water, and cans of Coke. Iacob points a calloused finger towards our yard below.

"Nice winch you got, on the front of your jeep. Buy that in Africa?" He speaks with his mouth full. The sight makes me think of pizza in a washing machine, whizzing round. Poor Iacob has hardly any teeth and eating can't be easy. Watching him isn't much fun, either.

"Actually," says Angela, "we bought that car in Romania."

"It used to belong to a hunter and the winch was already fitted," I add.

"Second-hand, then?" asks Titus, and we nod, munching away.

"Nice winch," says Iacob, "you could tow things with that."

"Call us if you need it," I say.

Iacob bites into his cheese pie. "I will, next time my cart is stuck in a ditch. You know how it is, sometimes, after a beer."

"Or three," says Titus, with a smirk.

"If I like a beer, now and then, so what, brother?"

"So that's why I can't take you with me to work abroad."

"Not that again." Iacob casts a hopeful look in our direction. Perhaps we can get him a job abroad, sometime. Or a beer, now.

"Drinks after the job is done, fair enough?" says Angela.

Iacob gives her a squinty wink. "*Mulţumesc*, Doamna."

I ask Titus about working abroad. He sips Coke and dabs his mouth with a napkin.

"Spain was first. I went in 2005 when I was 26. My friend was there and it sounded good, so why not? Next thing I know, I'm on a bus to Valencia. At the time, Romania was not in the EU and the Spanish border cops took me off the bus because I had no invitation or permit, only my reservation for a hotel."

"So, how did you get into Spain?"

"Some French guy offered to take me, for 150 euros. I put my bag in his car and we drove to a crossing that only locals used. I got out and walked over carrying just a little rucksack. There were no cops, nothing. The French guy followed me in his car, with my big bag in the back, and we hooked up again on the Spanish side."

"Quite easy, after all?" says Angela.

"Well, almost. I took a train to Barcelona then a bus to Valencia. When I got off the bus, my big bag had vanished. I grabbed a different bag and took a taxi to the hotel. In my room, I opened the bag. The clothes fitted me well and were better than mine."

Iacob stares at his brother. "You never told me that bit."

"Then what?" I ask.

Titus shrugs. "I looked for work on building sites, but I needed papers. Hotel living was expensive, so I rented a room in a house. After six weeks, I got my first job, renovating and building condos. At weekends, I'd go to the beach, visit the zoo and stuff."

"Save any money?" says Angela.

"I came home and built my extension, didn't I?" He points down the lane towards his pink cottage. There's our answer.

"Did you learn any Spanish?" I ask.

"Mostly from watching TV, and chatting on the street a bit."

"Did you mix with the locals?

"Not really," says Titus, "we Romanians stuck together. Bowling or billiards, we liked. The Spanish guys we knew, they seemed to prefer the bars and nightclubs."

Iacob grins. *Bars and nightclubs, eh.*

"Did you go to any bullfights?" I ask.

"Yes," says Titus, "they were beautiful."

"But violent, I think."

"Not really, bullfights are a Spanish tradition, like when we kill our pigs at Christmas."

"But you do that for food, not for sport."

"The Spanish eat the beef, Domnul Mike, and the bullring provides jobs." Titus pops an olive into his mouth and that's that.

"Did you hope to settle in Spain?" says Angela.

Titus shakes his head. "I knew it wouldn't last, so, no, not really. After five years, the crisis hit and I came home. The traffic here in Romania seemed so aggressive. In Spain, drivers are calmer, and from what I know, not so many drive after a drink. Not like here."

Titus glances at Iacob, who seems to have lost interest in the discussion and sits chewing in silence, gazing at our jeep. *I wonder how much he sees, with that squint?* It's rather severe, when you get this close. I'm also trying to remember the last time I saw him sober. Usually, he's prancing along our lane and gibbering to himself.

"You fancy Spain, Iacob?"

"Yes, Domnul Mike, sometime, maybe."

I glance at Titus, whose reaction says, *Sometime never.*

Angela pours more mineral water into our glasses. It hisses and bubbles, fizzes and pops. "Last summer you were in Italy, Titus?"

"Yes, Doamna Angela. I worked from 5 a.m. to 10.30 p.m., seven days a week for three months. I made 600 euros per month but came home to Romania with only 500 euros in savings. I'd spent most of my pay on food. I won't go back."

"They didn't feed you?"

"They provided board but little grub. The work was hard, so you had to eat a lot. I'd get through two loaves with every meal, but we were far from a supermarket and often I couldn't find any bread. I'd be working hungry."

"That's pretty bad. What sort of job?"

"I was looking after more than a hundred cows, sheep, pigs, all sorts. Some of the Romanian lads would arrive, see the size of the farm, and get straight back on the bus. *We didn't sign up for this.*"

"How were your managers, apart from stingy?"

"The Italians were bad, sometimes. They'd make us sleep by the road, at night. Bossy, too. I walked off one job after a row about a tractor."

"The one you crashed, hah! That bit, I remember," says Iacob.

"I never crashed it, brother, I just wasn't very good at it. No experience, see. I warned my boss. Even so, he insisted and I worked all day, ploughing a big field. But, when he saw my work, he refused to pay me. He got angry. Ready to hit me, he was."

"So, you left?"

"No, I pointed to a pitchfork and said, *See that, Mister?* He got the message. I might be small, but I'm not scared of anyone. I learned this as a kid. That's what to do with a bully. The sooner they know it, the better. Like that guy who owned the tractor." Titus slurps his Coke.

"What did he do?"

"He paid up, and I left. I'd had enough. Poles are lazy, too."

"I thought your boss was Italian?" says Angela.

"Correct."

"So, who was Polish?"

"Some of the workers in the fields. Good pie, this. If I could've eaten so well in Italy, I'd still be there. But not in a tractor."

"Have more," says Angela, and Iacob reaches for a third slice.

For pudding, we devour strawberries and ice cream. Iacob eats with his eyes closed. Bliss.

"Come and pick up strawberries, that's another con," says Titus.

"How so?" says Angela.

"Those bosses will say, *Yes, you should come, it's good pay per punnet!* So, you agree and they drive you to their fields. But the fruit is tiny and the punnets are *this* big and you work all day for 1.40 euros per tray. It's slave labour."

"Will you go back to Italy?"

"Probably, yes, but not to those damned fields. My mate says he can get me a job in an abattoir. I don't mind a bit of blood."

Titus chews a strawberry and looks at the mountains. I wonder what he's thinking. This is a nice place to live but he can't survive here, not with a wife and two kids in that pink cottage.

"Back to work," says Titus. He wipes his hands and stands up. *"Sărut mâna pentru masă,* Doamna Angela."

It's perhaps one of the nicest expressions in Romanian: *I kiss your hand, for the meal, Madam.*

Iacob rises to his feet with a weary sigh. *"Sărut mâna."*

"My pleasure," says Angela.

We go down to the yard with them to look at the wooden platform. Titus walks around it for a bit then crouches down and rubs his bristly jaw, eyeing the angles.

Iacob watches and waits. "So, Domnul Mike, what about you? What sort of book are you writing?"

Stretch Your Body

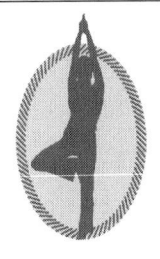

"Dear ladies, if you'd like a free yoga session, please contact me." Angela looks up from her phone. "How does that sound, Mike?"

"Short and sweet. Send it."

She thumbs the screen. "Message sent. Now we wait."

Then again, why wait? We pitch the proposal when we're out and about. Most of the women we meet shake their heads, move on, and we can guess why. Yoga means sex cult means Bivolaru, the weirdo who gave it a bad name in Romania, years ago. Some women, however, seem intrigued by Angela's offer, and, finally, we get lucky in a supermarket queue, down town in Dumbrăvița, when we meet two of our neighbours, Ionela and Iulia.

They're wearing tracksuits and listen closely as Angela explains what yoga is, what it isn't, and how it might help them. She even mentions the prince of darkness – lest they're wondering – and assures them she's no disciple of the infamous Bivolaru.

Little by little, their icy concerns about him thaw to a trickle of curiosity about Doamna Angela, then melt to a flood of interest in the well-proven and widely-acknowledged health benefits of yoga.

"Good for back pain, you say?" asks Ionela.

"Works wonders, ask Mike," says Angela, and I nod, on cue.

"Well, then," says Iulia, "if it's free, sign me up."

"And me," says Ionela.

Back home, we peruse Angela's list of names. It's getting longer, day by day. A few of them I know, most I don't, but something doesn't add up. The math, is what.

"Ten? Our terrace will only fit four or five, Angela."

"I'll offer two sessions, once the weather improves."

But the weather doesn't improve. What it does, in the mountains, is change rapidly: clear skies cloud over in fifteen minutes and you're running for shelter from a thunderstorm. Nor is it just about staying dry – it's also about staying alive.

One morning at breakfast, we hear on the radio that lightning has fried a flock of fifty wet sheep, overnight. It's hard to believe. One minute, you're in a field, ruminating on life in general, next minute you're dead and gone, up in smoking wool?

"Poor sheep." I reach for a slice of toast. Actually, maybe not.

Out walkies with the doggies, we come across a huge tree reduced to a charred and shattered stump. It makes you wonder what a lightning strike would do to a person. You can push your body, sure, but don't push your luck, not up here.

"If I were you, I'd hold on the outdoor yoga, Angela."

"You can say that again," she says.

So I do, but she doesn't laugh. She just stares at the stump.

Early summer brings a week of welcome sunshine. We check the weather forecast. Angela calls her yoga clients, arranges a session, and lays out the mats on our wooden deck. Two days running, she cancels the session because of gathering clouds and distant booms. We stand at our window, glum-faced, watching the sky.

"Someone up there doesn't want yoga down here, Mike."

"Now you sound like what's-her-name, the lady at the church. The councillor's wife who tried to dissuade us?"

"Miruna. Maybe she was right."

"Wrong. Everything comes to those who wait, you'll see."

"Wait how long, Mike? This wasn't such a good idea, after all."

"Angela, it's a great idea. Summer's out there, somewhere. It's coming to Culmea and so is yoga."

On the day of Angela's inaugural class – the first ever yoga session in our village, it seems – the gods are smiling, be they Hindu or Transylvanian. The sky is a lovely blue and the grey clouds have gone wherever clouds go. Our wooden terrace is warm and inviting and the breeze is just right. Even our cats seem to sense something is up – they prowl and purr, yawn and stretch, as we roll the yoga mats flat. Perhaps they'll join in.

The cowbell jangles above our front door, right on time, and Angela peeps through a window. "Four ladies, not bad."

Ionela, Iulia, Beatrice, and Regina look apprehensive as they enter our house, glancing with nervous grins at the Indonesian mask in the hall.

"Scary," says Regina, easing off her boots.

Their clothes are hardly suitable for yoga, despite Angela's advice about *loose and comfortable.* Three of the women are middle-aged and considerably overweight, presumably from diets high in meat, dairy, and treats. Cake Central, is Culmea. Beatrice looks red-faced already, from the walk. Ionela, on the other hand, is a human dipstick; six foot tall and skinny with it.

Angela leads them through the house to the terrace at the back. They stare at the yoga mats and giggle like little girls. It's a sweet moment, considering their age range is, what, forty-five to sixty years old? Angela stands at the front in her stretchy togs.

"Welcome, ladies, thank you for coming. Iulia, if you just could move your mat a bit to the left? Thanks, perfect. And Regina, to the right? Yes, great. OK, everyone, ready?" Angela presses her palms together, bows her head, and says, "*Namaste.*"

They stare, and Doamna Regina says, "What?"

"It means, *I bow to you,*" says Angela, "it's just a traditional greeting, people say it in India sometimes. Say it, if you like."

"Is it true they're all vegetarians?" says Ionela.

"Because of Hindu religion?" says Beatrice.

"Or so we heard, from Doamna Miruna," says Iulia.

"Not all of them," says Angela, "but quite a lot, yes."

"Is yoga a religion?" asks Ionela.

"Not for me," says Angela, "we'll just stretch and… Mike?"

"Yes?"

"Go away, please."

"Oh, sorry, I forgot. Best of luck, everyone."

As I retreat, Guru Angela is telling the ladies to try and copy her moves, as best they can. *I'll just show you some gentle stretches, no need to push ourselves too hard.* Hah, little do they know.

I'm sitting at my desk when the cowbell jangles again. It's Doamna Raluca, and she's brought her young son Emil. He looks flushed with excitement and carries a yoga mat tucked under his arm.

"A tourist left it in our guest house, Domnul Mike."

He kicks off his trainers, saunters through the house, and points. "Mama, they've already started. Told you we'd be late."

I open the sliding door onto the terrace. "Two more, Guru."

Angela looks puzzled to see young Emil. So much for *Ladies Only*. But she relents, because rules are meant to be broken, just like backbones. I chance a peek at her other clients. The stout women of Culmea are sprawled on their yoga mats, legs akimbo and faces contorted in mock agony. *My God, this is hard.*

Indian music drifts through the house – sinewy sitar lines and the gentle *dup-dup* of tabla drums. Sounds like the hard part is over and Angela has nudged her novices into meditation mode. By now, they'll be flat on their backs and relaxing. I leave my desk and sneak into the kitchen to brew a cup of tea.

Something groans on our sofa. It's one of the ladies. She is lying face down, head buried in cushions. I ask if she'd like a glass of water. She shakes her head, turning sideways to look at me. It's Doamna Beatrice. Her face is the colour of a lettuce. The inside of a lettuce. I'm wondering what to offer next. Perhaps an ambulance? I look up. Angela is gesturing at me from the terrace outside. *Don't worry, she'll be OK.*

The yoga session ends late in the afternoon. Most of the women look relaxed and happy. Serene, even.

"That was amazing," says Ionela, "I'm glowing all over."

"Same here, I liked the meditation bit best," says Regina.

"Had no idea yoga would be like that," says Iulia.

Raluca ties up her unruly hair. "Me neither, I always thought yoga was, you know, a bit–"

"Bivolaru?" says Angela.

The three women nod, and look a bit embarrassed.

"Mama, what's Bivolaru?" says little Emil.

"Never you mind," says Raluca, "let's go and milk the cows."

Doamna Beatrice is the last to leave. Angela takes her hand and says, "Feeling better?"

Beatrice nods. "Yes, not so bad now, thanks."

"Would you like a lift?" I ask.

"No, I prefer to walk, it's not far. The fresh air will help."

"I'm sorry if the yoga made you unwell," says Angela.

"Not your fault, Doamna Angela. It was the pork chops. Came back up, they did. I forgot about not eating too much beforehand." Beatrice reaches for a shoe. "Sorry I conked out."

At the door, she presses her palms together and inclines her head. *"Namaste."*

Angela bows. *"Namaste."*

Gorgeous Music

What if they fall? We pause, during a hike through the steep-sided gorge, to gawp at three rock climbers clinging to the sheer wall of grey limestone; they're high above us, tiny as flies on a window. The climber in the red singlet has a blond ponytail that swings side to side. *Woman or man?* A wiry arm reaches into a bum-bag and we glimpse a wisp of white. Chalk dust, probably, for a better grip.

"Don't worry," says our guide Gertrude, as if reading our minds, "they're on a rope."

She brushes a lock of silver hair from her tanned forehead. Her pale blue eyes scan the cliff, then she marches away, baggy shorts flapping and calf muscles flexing. Our stocky and resolute leader has little time for distractions on the trail. My wife and I linger awhile to ogle the human limpets.

"They're at least a hundred metres up," says Angela.

"Looks like fun."

"Not to me, Mike."

The farther we walk into the gorge, the cooler it gets. An icy breeze blasts into us, chilling our bones. Sedimentary rock soars skywards, to our left and right, and contains the most remarkable arching folds. We're in the petrified linen cupboard of the gods. It's ancient and a little creepy. Gertrude points her walking stick at steep slopes, high in the distance.

"Two mountain goats on that ledge, see?"

All I can see are trees. I need binoculars. *Next time.*

Our narrow path widens, and we reach a steep ravine lined by fir trees growing at weird angles.

"Have you ever seen that movie *Cold Mountain?*" says Gertrude. We nod, and she points ahead. "They filmed the ending up there. That scene when Nicole Kidman shoots her boyfriend, by mistake? The British actor, what's-his-name. Jim someone."

"Jude Law," I say.

"Yes, that's the one, he played the soldier home from war."

"Inman. Although the book is better, to be honest."

Angela chuckles. *You geek, to be honest.* Gertrude waves her stick like a wand. "We used to see bits of white stuff floating here, for months afterwards, they used so much fake snow."

"That's show biz."

"And the last thing we needed, Mike, in our national park."

We move on, scanning the ground for Tinseltown souvenirs.

Walking by a fast stream flowing through a deep gulley, we watch the water cascade over rocks and fallen tree trunks glazed with bright green lichen. Gertrude tells us that two young sweethearts drowned, a few years back, in a flash flood.

"Right here. No chance. Dangerous place."

The stream pops and gurgles, as if to concur.

At the next bend, we peruse a laminated board offering information for visitors. It has photos of numerous plants, rock formations, goats, bears, wolves, and even an amber-eyed lynx with pointy ears. The gorge's vital role in Hollywood history has been omitted, however, which seems a pity. Tourism, and so on?

"Wow, nice cave, up here." Angela walks on, beckoning me.

Leaving Gertrude to browse the blurb about flora and fauna, we reach a dome-shaped recess in the rock wall, about five metres high and ten metres wide. Perfect for a film about Neanderthals.

Angela squats on her heels. "Great place to stage a play, this."

"Looks like The Hollywood Bowl, same shape." I walk into the cave and clap my hands. The echo cracks back, sharp and clear. "Hear that, Angela? Excellent acoustics. Great place for a concert, ideal for a band."

"With you in it, by any chance?"

"One day, maybe. Safer than rock climbing."

"Perhaps we could invite a choir."

"A string quartet would be nice, too. Do we know anyone?"

"We could ask around. It's a nice venue. Or it could be."

"Right on our doorstep, too. Easy for us to set something up. It might work."

We lock eyes, and we just know it will. We pace in circles, talking over each other. Bright ideas bubble faster than a spring flood and by the time our guide ambles into the cave, we have a plan and a reason to wave our sticks.

"We want to organise a concert, right here, in the gorge."

"We'll call it *Gorgeous Music*. What do you think, Gertrude?"

Like many a whimsical notion, once shared, ours takes on a life of its own. Over the next few weeks, word spreads around the village. Most of the local adults seem unimpressed with our offer of a free concert in their ancient gorge, but we keep hearing echoes of it, albeit somewhat distorted by the time they reach us.

One sunny afternoon, a freckled teenager in a hay cart tells us that a famous Romanian rock band will soon play in the gorge, but he's not sure when. Days later, a wizened shepherd warns us it will be too cold down there for the orchestra. That evening, a tiny girl pedals her battered bike up our darkening lane to ask if we've heard about the disco. "For dancing, in the gorge," she adds.

Despite such glorious rumours and the expectations that feed upon them, we inch towards something more realistic, thanks to friends who want to help rather than gossip.

Gertrude and her husband Walter promise to bring clients from their guest house as a core audience. Mountain guide Hanno will bring his drums to accompany whoever. Our mutual friend Elsa, a retired actress who summers at her large home in Culmea, will bring a troop of German scouts from North Rhine-Westphalia. They'll be visiting her and know lots of campfire songs.

Best of all, Elsa has contacted an opera singer who will perform free at *Gorgeous Music*. She shares her suggestions by email, gushing goodwill, and it's classic Elsa – the ultimate social networker and gracious hostess of exuberant cultural soirées – but even so, we can hardly believe our iPads.

"An opera singer?" says Angela, wide-eyed.

"We're really onto something here."

"Certainly coming together, after just a few weeks."

"Imagine if we spent six months contacting artistes and sponsors?"

"We could stage *Gorgeous Music* every year."

"Apply for a permit. Charge admission. Pay performers. Cover our costs, maybe even donate something to the National Park."

"We should talk to the council, what do you think?"

"They'd welcome us with open wallets – *where's our cut?*"

Angela sets her iPad aside. "I say we focus. What about you?"

"Me?"

"Will you play at *Gorgeous Music?* I think you should. Our idea, after all."

"Agreed, but one guitar is with my luthier and the rest are in storage in the UK."

"Thought you might say that. Can't you borrow?"

On the day of the concert, the guitar I'm carrying down to the gorge seems unlikely to emit gorgeous music. The neck is dodgy, the strings are past it, and the tuning pegs are stubborn. A wily junk shop owner might tease a guitar like this from a top shelf – *because it's worth quite a bit, apparently* – just in case you're dim enough. Nevertheless, we have nice weather for a concert, so I'll try my best. The leaves rustle and the winding dirt road is striped with sunshine. Four more kilometres to walk. So far, so good.

An open-top BMW with Bucharest plates trundles towards us. Two young men sit upfront and two young women sit in the back. All of them wear sunglasses, all of them are smoking. Romanian rap music pumps from the audio speakers. The car stops and one of the women photographs some lambs in a nearby field. The lambs bolt from the din, spring-heeled, their hind legs kicking air.

We greet the tourists as we pass. Angela tells them a free concert in the gorge will start in about an hour. The driver flicks ash and says, "Actually, we know the guys who organised it." He drives on, smiling, and Angela smiles at me. Success has many parents. Our baby is up and running. We continue downhill.

By the time we reach the gorge, a blanket of ominous grey cloud has filled the sky. A dozen or so hikers mooch around the car park chatting in French, English, and who knows what. They wear rainproof tops, Lycra leggings, and serious-looking boots. Most carry little knapsacks, but some are strapped into rucksacks as big as barrels. One fellow sports a black watch studded with buttons that can probably tell him all sorts. The woman alongside him flaps her arms under a waxy yellow cape and has a sou'wester hat, as if ready to sail the north Atlantic in search of cod. Better safe than sorry, I suppose. If it rains she'll be dry, not drenched.

Angela leans towards me. "Not many locals, then?"

I scan the gathering for a familiar face but our neighbours are conspicuous by their absence. A few of the village kids are scrambling in the scree, nearby. Nice of them to come. They wave down at us and I raise a thumb.

"Let's hope Gertrude turns up, Angela."

"I'm sure she will. We're early. All these tourists are probably from her guest house. Can you hear singing? Listen."

"Sounds like angels, perhaps our time is up."

The voices rise and fall. Louder and louder. Teenage boys lope around the bend in the road. They're wearing identical grey shirts, striped neckerchiefs, and grey shorts. They're chanting in unison and slapping their thighs. Germans, by the sound of it.

"Probably the scouts," says Angela. "Is that Elsa at the back?"

A tall and stately matriarch in a scarlet shawl walks behind the group, chatting to a gangly blond scout and gesturing at the cliffs. She spots us and strides forward for friendly hugs – *mwah, mwah, so glad to be here* – then points, with a proud smile, at her recently-arrived guests.

"Zey walk more zan one hundrett and forty kilometre!"

We watch the scouts, in awe. Their chunky socks are rolled down and their boots are dusty. Elsa tells us they are hiking from Sibiu to Brașov for an endurance award. Actually, with their sun-bleached hair, deep tans, and pearly smiles, these handsome lads look as if they've just walked out of *Vogue*.

They amble on, with a weary swagger, into the gorge. A few of them trade banter and friendly punches. A tight unit, I bet, thriving on camaraderie and a shared goal. But their uniforms, bright badges, and daggers on lanyards look rather militaristic and get me thinking. About history. About how, eighty-five years ago, back in the 1930s, all scout groups in Germany were banned. Instead, many youngsters joined the only youth organisation allowed. They sang from a different repertoire and wore shirts of pale brown. We're lucky those days are gone. These cheery lads just want to conquer distance, not people. Time passes, time heals.

Gertrude arrives in a Land Rover. Her husband Walter, a broad-chested giant with a high forehead and a friendly manner, hops down from the passenger seat and opens the rear door. He summons the tourists who gather around as he plucks cases of juice and beer from the car. The tourists carry the cases along the narrow path into the gorge, following the scouts. We bring up the rear, chatting with Elsa, Walter and Gertrude, pausing to gaze at a tiny figure inching across the cliff face, high above us. Even the scouts seem impressed, craning their necks to watch.

Someone punches my arm. "What's up, asshole?"

It's Hanno, the flame-haired, green-eyed, Transylvanian Saxon mountain guide; self-proclaimed free spirit, former test driver, and eternal soul brother. When he's not in a tent up some remote valley, he's in a tent up the next one. But today he's here, all grin and goatee beard, and I'm delighted. Hanno shoves a drum at me. "Brought my snare, like you said. Let's rock, motherfucker."

"Good to see you, Hanno. Ever tried rock climbing?"

"Never mind that. We need to decide on songs. We're playing after the *Pfadfinder*, by the way. I already told them. They agree."

"After the who?"

"Not *The Who*. The *Pfadfinder*. It's German, means scouts."

"Oh, them? Right, whatever."

"They'll perform first because their songs are crap."

"What if ours are worse?"

"Shut up. Listen. We'll play some Hendrix, like that time at the guest house, ок? And maybe some Muddy Waters."

"I had a better guitar that time. Seen this one?"

Hanno squints at the junk shop relic and rubs his tufty beard.

"Make a nice fire later on, that will." He punches my arm, harder this time. "We can start with *Hey Joe*, what do you think?"

"Hardly party music."

"Who cares, it's Hendrix. Let's walk."

We continue along the path, planning our tunes. Hanno wants to start with Hendrix, followed by Hendrix. Elsa turns towards us and says the *Pfadfinder* sing very well. Hanno rolls his eyes at me.

"And the lady from Brașov?" says Angela.

Elsa's smile fades. "The lady from Brașov?"

"Your friend the opera singer, you said she would–"

"Ah, yes, but ze problem is …"

Gorgeous Music begins an hour late, as all good shows should because artistes must keep the audience waiting and build the atmosphere. Except in this case, the artistes must wait while the audience dawdles in the gorge, photographing climbers and gawping at distant, high-altitude herbivores. Perhaps we need posters and a new name: *Goatstock.*

Eventually, we arrive at the cave, about thirty people in total plus two stray dogs that know a snack when they smell one. The scouts squat on boulders, hugging tanned knees. According to Hanno, they would prefer not to perform first, so we will. Walter and Gertrude distribute free drinks. Elsa apologises, yet again, for the lack of opera singer who is unlikely to turn up, what with dying from a broken heart, onstage, forty kilometres away in Braşov, every other night. That's show biz. Perhaps we should've sent her a contract. Delivered in person. By a bear.

The sun is long gone and the air feels colder by the minute. Hanno and I stand in front of the cave, which, in the grey light of dusk, now looks less like The Hollywood Bowl and more like a damp den in a cliff. *I wonder if the rock climbers know any tunes?* Perhaps they could scurry up and abseil down, singing Hallelujah.

Angela makes a brief announcement, welcoming everyone to the inaugural *Gorgeous Music.* Heads nod and smiles glimmer. Restless children wander about, oblivious. Hanno gives me the eye, whacks his drum, and we launch into our version of *Hey Joe*. We sound abysmal. I'm not much of a singer. Even the dogs stare, tails tucked, incredulous. Hendrix must be turning in his pup tent.

When we finish our first song, the applause is polite rather than enthusiastic. So much for St Jimi. Then again, perhaps starting with his song about a murderous cuckold was not such a gorgeous idea.

"Bob Marley," says Hanno, which sounds like a better one, and we launch into *I Shot The Sheriff*, whilst tourists munch sandwiches and doggies lurk for scraps. The German scouts look bored out of their woggles. A little boy plants himself before us, picking his nose. He looks a bit worried. For us, probably.

"Light My Fire," says Hanno, and I wish someone would.

Our upbeat version of The Doors' brooding anthem gets a few boots tapping. It also sparks a timely memory, for me at least. It's all coming back: once upon a Christmas, I was a skint student busking with friends in dripping wet Wales and learned a vital lesson in stagecraft: it doesn't much matter what you play, as long as it makes your audience happy and they see you having fun. Because happiness is a virus, it's the bug of bugs, for which there is no known cure. People want fun, lively tunes. In other words, Hanno and I must woo the crowd, starting with this bored kid.

"Hey, Hanno, let's do *Old MacDonald's Farm*."

He gawks at me like a climber without a rope. "What the *f*–"

"We need something upbeat. It might work. Count us in."

Hanno rolls his eyes, taps his drumsticks, and we're off, *Ee-eye, ee-eye-oh!* The little boy extracts his finger from his nostril and does a little dance. A girl in a baseball cap skips from the audience to join him. *Elder sister, perhaps.* Their parents follow, bobbing left and right in heavy boots. More adults and youngsters merge alongside, including the kids from our village, to swell the numbers. A German scout rises to his feet, clapping and whistling; Angela shakes a tambourine; Hanno adds rim shots that crack and echo; Elsa whoops; Gertrude blows a kazoo, and Walter raises a can of beer, *Cheers.* The hiking path is soon packed with dancing people. We're cooking. It's hardly rock 'n' roll, but they like it. Well, most do; some of the adults huddle in chat, too preoccupied to participate, but never mind.

We segue into our last tune – a skiffle version of *Wheels On The Bus,* and Hanno looks ready to jump under one. Nevertheless, he performs a defiant, ear-popping drum solo to round us off then raises his sticks and beckons the boy scouts. "Follow that, ladies."

The *Pfadfinder* gather in the cave and ask us to accompany their performance. Hanno hammers an infectious beat and they pitch into a campfire song. It has three chords, a catchy chorus, and is easy for me even on this cranky guitar with ideas of its own. The German tourists warble along and the kids jig in circles.

The scouts sing half a dozen ditties, by which time the light is fading. For their rousing finale, they're slapping their chests, punching the air, and hollering sweet harmonies. *About what, I wonder?* Maybe I'll ask, later.

You know it's time to stop when the stray dogs leave. Our inaugural concert is finished. We amble as one, back down the path, towards the car park. Angela and I chat with Karl, a blue-eyed scout who likes the people and countryside of Transylvania. I tell him I liked that last song. "But what was it about, Karl?"

"About being with nature." He stoops to pick up some litter, tucks it into a pocket, and looks around. "We're in a very special place. I'm very glad I am here."

"So are we, thanks for singing."

We shake hands and Karl trots ahead, bow-legged, to catch up with his colleagues. Angela links my arm.

We're stragglers at the rear of the group and it feels right.

"So, next year?" I ask, hoisting the guitar onto my shoulder.

"Who knows, Mike? But I doubt it, somehow."

"Pity, it seemed such a good idea at the time."

"Agreed, but this gorge is too damp and cold, even in–" She stops and stares. "What's up with Elsa, why is she coming back?"

Elsa strides towards us, waving and yelling. People move aside to let her through. She's upset. Forgotten her bag or dropped her phone, perhaps. Actually, no, she's not upset. Ecstatic, more like.

"Angela! Mike! Delia iz here, look!"

A woman emerges from the gloom. She's dressed all in black and stepping carefully. She's of medium height, middle-aged, and striking-looking. A bright headscarf frames her oval face. Her eyebrows arch in perfect semi-circles like little caves. She's beaming at us, offering a gracious hand. Talk about charisma. Talk about presence. Star quality, or what. In fact, guess what. Elsa's glowing grin says it all. *Guess who.*

"I am so very, very sorry. Caught in traffic, you see!" Delia speaks perfect English and sounds rather posh. Her scintillating smile could enchant the back row of a theatre. We're smitten, garbling a welcome. *No problem, we understand, and thanks anyway.*

Delia looks past us. "So, please tell me, how was the concert? I do apologise. Am I really too late? Is everyone going home?"

We can only nod. Everyone is gone. They're just smudges of colour now, fading down the path and into the clammy night.

Delia sighs. "Such a pity. But, may I see the stage, at least?"

Elsa offers her a supporting arm and we walk slowly back to the cave. On arrival, Delia's eyebrows rise in unison. "Oh, I see."

She glances about, pursing her ruby lips. Darkness inches like black lichen down the limestone crags. *La Scala* this ain't.

"Iz going to rain," says Elsa, "so, perhapz next time?"

"Certainly, if there is a next time," says Delia, wistfully. She looks at me. I'm racking my repertoire for an opera aria I can play. Fat chance of that, and I doubt Delia will sing *Old McDonald*. But wait a minute, there is one song. "Do you know *Summertime?*"

"Of course, Mike."

"Great, what's your key?"

Delia clears her throat and hums the melody. I run fingers up the guitar's neck until I find her root note and my chord. She's in A flat minor and we're about to be entranced, I just know it.

"Ready, Delia?"

"Yes, let's."

Raindrops patter on the path as we step into the cave. It's icy cold but Delia's voice is hotter than July. Angela and Elsa huddle together, swaying gently. I've got goose-pimples – or perhaps goat pimples – and am so enthralled to be accompanying a professional opera singer that I fluff my E flat 9 and Delia winces at me: *Ouch, wrong chord.* We press on regardless. Rain drifts down in silver clouds, the living is easy, and our song ends all too soon, just like summer. Applause echoes from a bright yellow blob in the distance, way down the path. *The woman in the cape?* Someone whistles.

Someone yells in German. Probably the scouts. And that was that.

"Delia, one more song!" cries Elsa, clapping wildly.

Delia gives a little bow and launches into *Ave Maria*. I don't even try to play along. I just listen. I'm lucky to be here. Her voice weaves a magic spell. I know this song. Schubert wrote it, after reading a poem by Walter Scott, whose Scottish highland maiden sought refuge in a goblin's cave. And here we are, in a cave. *Imagine that.* It's all too much. The song is too beautiful. I could weep. I want a kilt. Delia hits her high note. It could shatter glass. My god, what a voice. We could do this every summer, why not? *Yes, let's.* Every summer until the angels sing. We found one.

My wife squeezes my arm and murmurs, "Gorgeous music."

Heavens Above

Our young neighbour Dragoș wobbles down the lane, strapped into a heavy rucksack almost as big as himself. Arms out for balance, he lurches along like a miniature astronaut exploring a new planet. Heaven knows what's in that backpack – his rocket manual? Encyclopædia Britannica? You have to wonder, seeing as he's only six years old and can hardly read or write. Talk about excess baggage.

Any minute now, he'll peep through our fence, big brown eyes scanning the yard, left and right. Yards are interesting, especially other people's. He'll spot me kneeling down with my hammer and nails and he'll want to know why. *Should I tell him the painful truth?* Maybe not, since Dragoș has a fertile imagination and who knows where that might lead. Then again, perhaps I will, if he asks; he's a country kid with few illusions. It might help to save a life or two. Here he comes.

"Domnul Mike, what are you doing down there?"

"Hi, Dragoș, I'm blocking holes under our fence."

"Holes?"

"To stop hedgehogs."

"With a hammer?"

"And some nails and twisty wire, see?"

"Oh, yes. But why are you stopping hedgehogs?"

"Because our dogs caught a big one and they woke us up at 3 a.m. They were barking a lot."

"Domnul Mike."

"Yes, Dragoș?"

"A hedgehog can roll into a ball. Did it roll in a ball?"

"Yes, but that didn't help."

"How do you mean?"

"Well, I took it to the vet this morning and he put it to sleep."

"Domnul Mike."

"Yes, Dragoș?"

"Hedgehogs sleep every day. So, why did you need the vet?"

"Because it was hurt. Our dogs bit it."

"Hurt bad?"

"Pretty bad, yes. Very bad, in fact."

"Will the hedgehog get better when it wakes up?"

"No, Dragoș. When it wakes up, it will be in heaven."

Dragoș frowns. No further questions. But then again.

"Domnul Mike?"

"Yes, Dragoș?"

"That aeroplane we were talking about, last week? The one that went missing? I know what happened."

I rise from my knees and squat on my haunches. "Really?"

Dragoș nods. "It crashed. Sixty-three people went to heaven."

"Oh, that's terrible. Are you sure? Was it on the news?"

"Sixty-three, Domnul Mike."

"But I thought that plane was quite small, with two seats?"

Dragoș shrugs. "It must have crashed into a bus queue."

"Ah, yes, maybe. In Brașov, perhaps? Or Sibiu, d'you think?"

Dragoș nods. "Somewhere like that."

"Those poor people. Perhaps it will be on the radio, later."

"Domnul Mike."

"Yes, Dragoș."

He adjusts his heavy rucksack, and points. "Your red cat is on the roof."

I turn to see. Dragoș is right about that, at least; ginger puss Roy is creeping across our garage roof and checking the mud nests that cling to the eaves of our house, one metre above his head.

"What is your cat doing up there?" says Dragoș.

"He's waiting to catch a bird."

"You should tell him to come down."

"I tried, but Roy doesn't speak Romanian or English."

"Because he's from Azerbaijan!" Dragoș grins.

"You remember."

"It's what you told me, Domnul Mike, when I showed you my kitten."

"So I did. I hope you've stopped washing her. Kittens don't need to be washed, remember? They wash themselves. Your kitten will catch a cold and go to heaven. How's she doing?"

"Kitten ran away, actually." Dragoș scratches his head then he rubs his nose. *Body language. Very interesting, actually.*

"Domnul Mike."

"Yes?"

"I have to go home. It's time to feed Ursulică."

"I thought you only feed your dog in the evenings?"

"Except for today."

"OK. Do you remember how we say Ursulică in English?"

"Little Bear."

"Smart lad."

"Bye, then."

"Bye, Dragoș."

He lumbers away in his jetpack but stops after a few paces. "Domnul Mike."

"Yes?"

He points at the fence. "There's a hole here. For hedgehogs."

Asta e

The fluffy puppy trots down the path from my neighbour's house, eager to make friends. *With me? Great.* It has a white face with big black smudges for eyes. Looks like a panda. Adorable. I crouch and click fingers in welcome. *Hello, little one.*

Eight-year-old Emil skips down the path, after the pup, grinning. "Hello Domnul Mike."

"Hello, Emil, *ce faci?*"

"Very-well-thank-you. See my new dog? Do you like it?"

"A lot, yes, lovely dog. Boy or girl?"

"Boy, of course." Emil ruffles the pup's head.

"And his name is?"

"El nu are încă un nume."

"No name, yet? Fair enough. You'll decide soon, I expect."

"Yes, soon."

We squat together and the pup nibbles at our fingers with tiny white fangs as sharp as toothpicks. I envy my young neighbour.

Boy and pup will grow up together and soon become man and dog. Best friends. It's a nice thought, but I'm wary.

"Hey, dog, no bite!" Emil jerks his hand away, giggling.

"You could call him *Panda*. Is that a good name?"

Emil shrugs. *"El nu are încă un nume."*

The pup rolls onto its back, paws akimbo. Tickle tummy time.

"He's very friendly, your pup. How long have you had him?"

"Tata buy him yesterday. My other dog was die. Remember?"

"Yes, of course. Bobiță was a nice dog. Poor Bobiță."

I stroke the new pup's distended belly. It probably has worms.

Emil gives me a quizzical look. "What means *poor* Bobiță?"

"Hmm, well, I suppose it means unlucky, unfortunate."

"Is that why Bobiță was die?"

I'm wondering how to respond. I could tell little Emil that poor Bobiță died because *Tata* did not phone the vet when the dog got sick. I could even suggest that poor Bobiță died of boredom after ten years on a chain. I could tell him that whoever severed half of poor Bobiță's ear, with a knife and no anaesthetic, had their head stuck up the arse of some ancient superstition. Instead, I'll repeat the convenient untruth that passes for pity in these parts.

"I just mean that poor Bobiță got sick and no one could help him, Emil. Perhaps he ate too much food, like your grandma said."

"Yes, too much food. That's what she said. Poor Bobiță."

"If this pup gets sick, you must phone the vet. Promise?"

"Promise."

"And your pup will soon need somewhere warm to sleep, in a kennel, for example."

"Yes."

"And you should probably take it for some nice walks. Dogs do not like to be tied up, day and night."

"Walks, yes. And a kennel. Did we forget anything?"

"And I hope nobody will cut his ear."

Emil frowns. Perhaps he doesn't understand. On the other hand, perhaps he's just confused because any fool knows you have to cut your dog's ear in half. Otherwise, it's not a proper dog. His mother calls down from the house. *Emil, hai să mâncăm!* She's leaning from a window, beckoning him. *Come and eat!* She spots me and waves. *Bună, Domnul Mike!* I wave back. *Bună, Doamna Raluca!* She yells again. "Emil, did you hear me?"

Emil bids me farewell and hoists the pup by its front paws. The pup squeals. Emil tucks it under his arm and strides up the slope.

My favourite vet huddles over a grey cat. It lies unconscious on his stainless steel table. Cosmin stands alongside, rising on the balls of his feet as he sews up the cat's tummy. Cosmin's got new shoes, by the look of it. New Balance, as ever. Pink and blue, these. Loves his trainers, our Cosmin. He stitches slowly and carefully, in and out, in and out. His black hair is streaked with grey and matches the moggy. His head is so close to the cat, he appears to be wearing a fur hat.

"Tricky, this, Mike. Now tell me again, you want what?"

"To know why shepherds cut their dogs' ears."

"Because they're fucking idiots. You ever see sutures as good as these?"

"No, but I can't help wondering."

"About my sutures?"

"About cutting dogs' ears, about why shepherds do it. Superstition, yes? Like putting a red rosette on a horse's bridle?"

"Actually, no. One old guy told me a dog's ear protects it from rain. He cut it off so his dog would sleep with that ear on the ground and hear any bears that came for his sheep."

"Bears wearing big boots, presumably?"

"Exactly. It's idiotic, like I said. And you came to ask me that?"

"And for worm pills. I'm going away for a bit and want to make sure my neighbour has some for his pup. You didn't see my text?"

"Text? Sorry, no. My watch won't sync. Not yet, anyway."

"Your watch?"

Cosmin pulls up the sleeve of his smock and raises his wrist. "Smartwatch. Like it?"

I look closer, at sleek steel and shiny black glass. "Very nice. Pity it doesn't work."

"It will, soon. Guess what? I can use it during surgery, like now. Voice-activated, this watch."

"You should be on *Star Trek*. You could be their vet. *Star Vet*."

"I wish. Anyway, give me five minutes, and I'll sort you out for worm pills. Any more questions, apart from the ear business?"

"No, I was just curious."

"Curiosity killed the cat, Mike."

"This cat is dead?"

"Fucking hope not."

Something beeps. Cosmin winks at me and says, "Yes, Mama?"

Smart, that watch.

A mountain bike zooms past me on the muddy lane, with just inches to spare. Startled, my dog leaps sideways and barks. The bike skids to a halt and the young rider turns around, looking back at us. He's blond and wearing reflective wraparound sunglasses.

"Domnul Mike, you're home?"

"Hello, Emil, Didn't recognise you there, for a moment. *Ce faci?*"

"Very-well-thank-you. How was in England?"

"Yeah, all good, thanks. Stayed with my mum for a couple of weeks. Played music in my brother's band, he had a party. Is that a new bike?"

"Yes, from Tata." Emil grins, dead proud. He looks cool in his funky shades. I spot myself, and Linda, reflected in each curved lens. We are distorted, warped and wobbly, like in a hall of mirrors.

"Nice day for a ride, then?" I gesture at the blue sky and green slopes but he seems to have other things on his mind.

"Domnul Mike, when is ukulele class?"

"Next week, probably. Have you been practising?"

"Of course."

"Good lad. Any problems?"

"E9, because you need to press hard. That chord hurts."

"It will get easier. How's your puppy, by the way?"

"Getting big. He's at home, probably sleeping."

"Did you give him those worm pills I brought?"
"Think so."
"Did you take him for a little walk?"
"Not yet."
"Does he have a name?"
"*Panda.* Because he looks like a panda. *Tata* said so."
"It's a good name."
"Domnul Mike, do you want to see Panda?"
"I'd love to."

When we reach their yard, Emil stashes his bike and disappears into the house. I stand and wait, hoping to catch a glimpse of his pup. Three brown hens scoot by, followed by a marauding cockerel whose feathers shimmer blue and gold. It pauses to eye my dog with disdain, then lets rip: *Cock-a-doodle-you.* Linda snaps and barks. *Come here and say that.* I pull her away and we explore the yard. It's a bit of a mess, as ever, and strewn with junk. Linda sniffs at rusty pots, cracked bowls, and long-forgotten toys encrusted with cow kak. I peep under benches and behind a huge water barrel. *No pup.*

No people, either. Perhaps Emil's parents are enjoying an afternoon nap. Perhaps they're down at the spring with their cows. *But where's little Panda?* Dogs are not allowed indoors so he must be out here somewhere. I whistle and call his name. No luck. Perhaps he's spotted Linda and is scared. I tie her to a post and move on alone.

I find the pup eventually, around the back of the barn, under a large wooden sled. He's a quivering bundle of black and white fur. Shiny eyes stare out at me. Panda eyes, in fact. It's a perfect name for a lovely little dog. I click fingers. *Ce faci, Panda?* But there's no welcome for me. He backs off, whining and pressing himself against the wall of the barn. He's not the friendly pup I met a month ago. Bigger, yes, but something has changed. He looks miserable: *Leave me alone.*

I try again, reaching under the sled to fondle his chunky paws. This time, Panda licks my hand. His tail thumps on the damp grass. Progress, indeed. His head is a smooth dome of white fur spotted with dark red paint. Panda has been having fun, by the look of it, nosing where he shouldn't. *Has someone been shouting at him?* I grip his yellow leather collar and coax him out. *Good boy, easy now.* Under the bright sun, I notice that one of Panda's ears is just a stump of cartilage. Some brute has cut the flap off. These dark spots on his head are not paint. They're bloodstains.

"Domnul Mike, unde sunteți?"

A shrill voice echoes from the yard – Emil's grandmother, by the sound of it. I walk back around to meet her, cradling the pup.

Doamna Regina waddles towards me, wearing a see-through top and no bra. Her breasts droop and sway. She extends her arms, and we embrace, somewhat awkwardly, with Panda between us.

"Mike, te-ai întors! Ce faci? Dormeam! Câinele tău m-a trezit!"

You're back, Mike. How are you? I was asleep! Your dog woke me up!

I smile and shrug. Presumably, she did not hear her cockerel.

"Sorry about the barking, Doamna Regina."

"No problem, Domnul! Nice holiday? Is your mum well?"

"All good, thanks, yeah. I see this little doggie has grown?"

"That thing? Yes, I'll say. Eats too much and howls all night."

"Doamna Regina…"

"Yes, Domnul Mike?"

"Someone cut off half of Panda's ear. How come?"

She avoids my gaze, shooing her busybody hens. *Tsk-tsk*.

"Doamna Regina?"

"Yes, Domnul Mike?"

"Who cut Panda's ear? Your pup was fine with two ears. That's how God made him, don't you think?"

Her thin lips arc down in a grimace. "Asta e, Domnul."

"*Asta e? That's how it is?* Doamna, who did this?"

"A shepherd from the village. Emil's *tata* phoned him to come."

"This was Domnul Radu's idea? But why? This is cruel, barbaric. Can't you see?"

Regina has no answer. She doesn't need one. That's how it is. She strides after her hens – *shoo* – and would probably like to shoo me, I bet. I should leave, and I will, but not just yet.

"Doamna Regina, hurting animals is wrong. Illegal, in fact. There are new laws to protect them, passed by Parliament. We live in Europe now, times are changing. Please, tell Radu that what his shepherd friend did to this little dog is not right. It's very bad and makes no sense. Even a vet says so, the same vet who sold me those worm pills for Panda. Remember?"

She gives me a look – uncomfortable but unconvinced. "I'll be sure to tell Radu what you said, Domnul Mike."

"Please do, *mulțumesc.* I'd be happy to discuss it with him."

Doamna Regina stares at me. Perhaps there should be a law to silence meddling foreigners. *Time to go.* I place Panda in her arms. The pup wriggles and whines. Doamna Regina drops him on the ground – *Yuk!* – then brushes invisible hairs from her top. I leave without another word, lest I blow mine. Young Emil is still indoors, probably zapping bug-eyed monsters on his laptop.

I sense Regina's disgruntled gaze on the back of my head as I tramp down the slope. Rain spits and swirls. I stalk home, dragged by my wet dog, with steam coming out of my ears. All two of 'em.

Angela is ironing clothes and listening to Bach, whose *Well-Tempered Clavier* soothes my sodden spirits, sort of. I peel off my sodden jacket and shove it on a hangar. She folds a bed sheet.

"Nice walk, Mike?"

"Not really."

"Quite a downpour, eh?"

"On the way back, yes."

"Where did you go today?"

"Top road. I met young Emil and stopped by their place."

"Actually, his dad just rang. He wanted a word with you."

"Radu wants a word with me? Let me guess, about their pup?"

"About a usb chip, actually."

"What?"

"Radu wants to try a usb chip. He's heard they're useful. I told him, *No problem, we have a few spare.* Is there a problem?"

I stare at my wet socks. The iron hisses. *That's how it is.*

Every Picture

It's all about capturing the moment, so I'd better be quick.

"Tanti Lina, may I take a photo?"

Our elderly neighbour turns towards me, raising a hand to shade her eyes from the sun. She squints towards the fence and seems confused. Perhaps she didn't hear. Deaf as this wooden post under my elbow, is Tanti Lina. I brandish my camera. Might help.

"A photo of you and your family cutting grass. May I?"

She shrugs. *"Ba da, Domnul Mike, cum să nu?"*

Sure, why not. Tanti Lina turns back to her family in the meadow, pointing here and there. She's telling them something about the grass, but no one replies. Her middle-aged daughter Gloria is thumbing a phone; her teenaged granddaughter Camelia is sharpening a scythe. The chubby guy in the pink polo shirt is staring at me.

Click.

I wave goodbye and amble home. *"Mulțumesc,* Tanti Lina."

"Cu plăcere."

Back in our kitchen, sipping tea, I scroll through some shots from my walk: a fierce-looking sheep with bizarre horns, an ancient wooden wheelbarrow, a tree blasted by lightning, a blur of brown in a blue sky – *that'll be the hawk.* None of them are much good, but my final effort – of Tanti Lina and company in the meadow – is not bad. If every picture tells a story, this one hints at the eternal rhythms of family life in a remote mountain village. At least, I hope so. It's got something, anyway. *But what?* I look closer.

In the background, a stark ridge of mountains; below it, dusky hills sweep down into emerald pastures that glisten like duckweed. The light is just right – sunny but not bleached. *Wish I knew why; I should probably check my settings and find out.*

In the foreground, stands Tanti Lina. She's in profile, headscarf knotted at her chin, sharp nose protruding. She's pointing at the grass: *Cut this patch.* Gloria is nearby in tight black jeans and a skimpy black T-shirt. A tall and slim brunette, she has dark, mysterious eyes, sharp cheekbones, and wears her hair piled high. Quite a rock star, in fact.

Young Camelia's cut-off denim shorts reveal hiker's legs, but pale as buttermilk. She's twisting sideways at the hips, gripping her scythe, ready to swing it down and across the grass.

At the far right, stands the middle-aged man in the pink polo shirt. I know the face but can't remember the name. *Domnul Bratto? Domnul Gupta?* He's staring at me as if he can't remember mine. His expression is hardly friendly but makes the photo more interesting, as does his posture: one hand tucked in a pocket, belly sagging over his belt. He's ignoring Tanti Lina, who does go on.

There's something else, too. Something about the perspective, and how the composition leads the eye from left to right. Perhaps I've cracked the Law of Thirds, albeit unwittingly. Whatever, I like this shot. *Put it on Facebook, see if anyone else does?*

I upload the photo and write a simple caption about neighbours cutting grass. I should probably tag them. *But who's Mr Pink?* I'll phone my wife. She'll probably know. Then again, she's at the dentist, for a difficult procedure, starting around now. I check my watch. Better be quick. I thumb her number and look at the man in my photos, trying to recall his name.

"They call him *Grasu*," says Angela, "why do you ask?"

"Nothing important. How's it going?"

"Your favourite dentist is checking my X-ray. Anything else?"

"No, sorry to bother you. Good luck, Angela, and say hello from me."

"Hello from me."

Back on Facebook, I tag the fellow in pink – *Domnul Grasu* – post my photo, then scroll down to look at others. A friend in Los Angeles has snapped her frothy coffee at the airport. A carpenter in Italy has contributed stylish bunk-beds painted yellow. Next, someone's shiny-nosed Labrador pup is chewing a cardboard box. You can see why people get addicted to social media.

Scrolling back up, I notice that my photo has received seven LOLS, and five thumbs. *Hmm, that was quick?* Maybe I'll contact National Geographic to ask if they need a freelancer in Transylvania.

Angela arrives home with a numb face and a worried look. "Dentist says six months to put this right. I hope he's wrong."

We sit in our armchairs with purring cats curled in our laps. Angela asks me about my day, but there's not much to say.

"I did some work, went for a walk. Put a photo on Facebook. Over a hundred likes, last time I checked. A record, for me."

"Pretty good, after just a few hours. What's in your photo?"

I show it to her, on my phone, and she seems impressed.

"Nice shot, good light, well balanced. Gloria looks amazing in black. I like how Tanti Lina is pointing. What's the caption? I need my specs."

She roots in her bag and I look at the photo. Perhaps I should turn pro, buy one of those big zoom lenses the size of a salami and a khaki bush vest with lots of pockets.

"You see, Angela, it's all about capturing the moment. Wow, check it out, one hundred and fifty *likes*, now. How about that? I've never had so many. Mostly from locals. They love this photo."

Angela puts her specs on and leans closer. "Not surprised."

"How do you mean?"

"Do you realise what you called the guy in pink?"

"*Grasu.* It's quite appropriate, seeing as they're cutting grass."

"Except that's not his name."

"You said it was."

"I said they *call* him Grasu, but that's just a nickname. You've tagged him *Domnul Grasu.*"

"What does it mean?"

"Mister Fatso."

Bright Spark

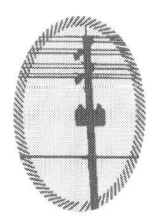

"Who's that, up our pole?" I point down the lane, shielding my eyes from the dazzling sunset over distant mountains.

A diminutive man clings to the electricity pole in the sloping field opposite our house. He's twenty feet up and hanging on for dear life. Our dogs strain at their leashes, gasping and whining. It's their pole, too.

"Whoever it is," says Angela, "he doesn't look safe."

"And what's he doing with those tools?" I ask.

"No idea."

"Must be from the electricity board. Power cut, maybe."

"But where's the van?" says Angela

"It's Domnul Vasile. I can tell from his black hat."

"You're right. Bit old to be climbing wooden poles, though?"

"Oh, my God, he's fiddling with the connections. He's tugging on that cable, see? He's risking his life, Mike."

"What a nit."

"Let's see what's going on."

Side by side, we trot down the lane, hopping ruts and rocks. The dogs lunge ahead, gasping and yipping.

As we enter the field, we spot half a dozen villagers standing behind a huge conical haystack. We nod, and they nod back, *Hello, hello.* They seem worried and turn away to look in the opposite direction, where the field slopes away into a steep valley; never mind Vasile up the pole with his pockets full of pliers and tufty grey head stuffed with bright ideas. He looks down at us and raises a thumb, as you do. *Afternoon, neighbours.* His leery grin lasts too long and I reckon I know why.

Tanti Lina stands, her arms folded, chatting with two other elderly ladies. They all wear headscarves and housecoats. Three men in T-shirts squat beside the haystack, sucking on cans of beer. Our neighbour Horia drags a large coil of robust cable across the grass. Looks like hard work, even for a big guy like him. One end of the cable is attached to a small mobile generator with rusty wheels. Rusty everything, in fact. The other end is attached to the bobbins at the top of the electricity pole. Or it will be, when his dad Vasile gets his act together. Father and son, eh? Laurel & Hardy, more like, or *Stan și Bran,* as Romanians say. I have no clue what they're up to but my wife might know, with her engineering background.

"What are they doing, Angela?"

"Jerry-rigging that mobile generator, I think."

"Not a generator," says Horia, lumbering towards us in a mucky white singlet and red cap. His round face is the colour of boiled beetroot. He should be in a cartoon, with steam coming out of his nose.

"Not a generator?" says Angela, apparently as puzzled as I am.

"Winch," says Horia, "and can you move these dogs of yours?"

We yank the dogs aside to let Horia pass. He tips his cap at my wife. "Sorry, I'm in a bit of a hurry."

"No problem," says Angela, "but what's the problem?

Horia pauses, breathing hard, biceps like rugby balls. "Cow."

"Excuse me?"

Horia points. "Down in the valley. My cow is stuck in a ravine. Pregnant too. Can't budge. Stuck fast and not happy about it."

"Oh, I'm sorry."

"Her fault, not yours. My fault, actually, I let her stray."

We look down the sloping field. It's a long, steep drop into the woods below. I can see treetops down there, but no ravine and no cow. "So, you're hoping to pull her back up with that winch?"

Horia shrugs. "That's the idea, or at least free her so she can walk. I've got three hundred metres of steel wire on the winch. The cow is at two-fifty, by my step. I strapped a harness on her. Got more cable here if we need it."

"Does your dad know what he's doing, up that pole?" says Angela.

"So he says."

"What if he falls?"

"He'd better not or I'll lose my cow. She's been down there since yesterday afternoon. By the time we borrowed the winch, we were too late to try. So, she was out all last night. Lucky a bear wasn't around. But a bear will get her scent tonight, that's for sure. Anyway, must hurry."

"Horia, I have an idea."

205

His smile suggests that, on the contrary, I have no idea. "Yes, Domnul Mike?"

"Our jeep has a winch at the front with a big hook. It used to belong to a hunter."

"And?" He pulls cable, hand over hand, uncoiling it loop by loop.

"We could park our jeep in this field and pull the cow up. Worth a try, at least? That way, your dad does not risk his life."

"Domnul Vasile shouldn't be up there, not at his age," says Angela.

Horia extends his lower lip. "How long, Doamna Angela?"

"Two minutes. The jeep is in our yard, just across the lane."

"I mean, how long is the cable on your *winch?*"

"Not sure, we've never used it."

"Great. And your jeep is that toy Suzuki thing, right?"

I nod. "Well, yes, it's pretty small. But quite strong."

Horia grins. "Any idea how much a pregnant cow weighs?"

"Not really."

"Didn't think so. Your jeep will end up in the ravine. Then what?" Horia smiles at us because he's smart and we're not. I look towards his winch. It's about the size of, what, a dustbin? Then I look towards our yard. *That toy Suzuki* is the size of four cows.

"Horia, you think our jeep weighs less than your winch?" I ask.

But someone is shouting, and we all turn. Vasile is waving down at us from the electricity pole.

"Horia! Try now, son! Start it up!"

Horia trots back to his rusty, trusty winch. He crouches beside it, pokes a button, and the machine growls into life. The steel cable flexes, goes taut, and the motor whines and rasps as it grapples with the weight of the huge cow, far below. The three men in T-shirts dump their beer cans and hold the winch steady. Our dogs hop in circles, spooked by the shrieking iron beast.

"Better get them home," says Angela, "we can't help, anyway."

We walk out of the field and past the electricity pole. Vasile clambers down it like an arthritic monkey and hops off. He loses balance in the rough grass and lunges into me, reeking of alcohol.

"I did it, Domnul Mike. But those bobbins are a bugger."

We do a little two-step towards the lane. He's grasping my arm and watching his feet like a novice dancer. "My lace is undone."

"You were risking your life up there," says Angela.

"Easy when you know how. Electrician, I was."

"Almost fried, you were. Have you been drinking, Vasile?"

"One or two, Doamna, I do apologise."

"Up a pole, fiddling with powerful wires, drunk?"

Vasile grasps her arm. "Hear that? The winch is working. So?"

"What you did was dangerous," I say. "You, of all people, should know better, Domnul Vasile."

Our elderly neighbour stands back, scowling. When you try to reason with a drunk, there's always a risk you'll say the wrong thing and it seems I have. He wags a finger at me, boozy eyes aflame. He steps forward, squaring up. *Wasn't Vasile a boxer, too?* He sways from side to side, adjusting his hat and racking his pickled brain for an appropriate rebuke. Here it comes.

"*Dangerous,* Domnul Mike? I'll tell you what's dangerous. Kissing a woman, that's what! Yes, kissing a woman. Because you never know where it will lead, do you? You never know where you'll end up. Like me, in this godforsaken… place."

Vasile glares at the dusky hills and stumbles off, muttering away and punching air. We watch and wonder, until he vanishes around the bend.

"Don't ask," says Angela, and I won't.

Remember Maya

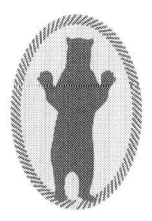

"Why did I *do* it? Actually, I don't like to explain, because every time, it makes me sad."

Cristina Lapiș faces our video camera, shoulders bunched against a breeze on the forest road. She wears a quilted black coat with a *fleur-de-lis* motif, jeans, and Timberlands. A slim woman in her mid-fifties, she has expressive brown eyes and full lips. Her black beret is tilted back revealing a strawberry blonde bob that frames her pretty face. She's Romanian but looks French, *très* Bardot. She sighs, and, eventually, concludes her answer. "A bear died in my arms. *That's* why I did it."

What Cristina Lapiș did was build a sanctuary, in 2005, for mistreated, captive brown bears. She started with two; now she has eighty-eight, and her sanctuary at Zărnești is regarded as the best of its kind in the world. It occupies seventy hectares of natural oak forest and meadows, divided into wooded enclosures, the biggest of which is six hectares.

"Come, let me show you around," Cristina says, strolling with Angela up the dirt road that winds through the woodland. "This video is for YouTube, I believe?"

"Yes," says Angela, "that's the idea, we're making a series of short documentaries about life in Transylvania. Thanks again for agreeing to the interview."

"My pleasure. The more people know about this place, the better. Although, I didn't always feel that way."

They move on, chatting, and I walk behind them with Cristina's husband. Roger is French, friendly but reserved, fine-boned with a deep tan, and strolls along with his hands clasped beside his back. He could be a diplomat on vacation. He wears a navy cagoule, jeans, and black hiking boots. I ask whether he's a veterinarian, environmentalist, or whatever.

"I'm a retired diplomat," says Roger.

I'm wondering how to reply, when I spot the bears. A dozen of them, keen-eyed and tracking our progress. They're lounging just a few yards away, on a grassy slope, behind the high steel fence.

The bears are big, brown and fluffy, as you'd expect. They're also very lucky to be here, which is probably something they didn't expect. Life was not always this easy. Truth is, life for them was pretty horrendous, all because of human beings. They gaze at a group of happy tourists coming the other way with a brunette guide in a fleecy green top. The guide warns everyone to keep their distance from the electrified fence. Cristina watches them for a moment, then turns back to Angela.

"Are we recording?"

"Yes," says Angela, "ready when you are."

Cristina nods towards the tourists. "I'm glad they're here now, but for the first two years after we opened, I refused to allow any visitors. These bears had suffered so much, you see, because of people who had locked them in cages for other people to gawp at. But one day, I realised something and had a change of heart. Come, I'll show you."

She leads us to a large billboard of information for visitors. A big colour photo of a brown bear looms above us. Cristina points up.

"So, this is Maya. After six years in a cage, she refused to go on living and ate her own paws. That's when we heard about her and intervened. Despite two surgical operations, she passed away, in my arms. Now, what I'll say next might sound childish, but it's true: I promised Maya, as she was dying, that no bear would suffer like this ever again."

Cristina pauses to wipe her eyes. Roger wraps a comforting arm around her. She nods, *I'm fine,* but takes a few moments to regain her composure before continuing.

"So, I knew I had to help. What I didn't know was how many bears lived in captivity and how much their owners would resist my efforts. I tried for seven years, before we built this place, to convince people that their bears should live in a forest. They didn't believe me. They'd rescued cubs from the forest – often after shooting their mothers for sport – and said the cubs were grown and happy. *In cages, really?*" Cristina shakes her head.

"So, how did you convince the owners?" I ask.

"It took time. Eventually, with help from local authorities here in Zărnești, we got a little piece of land and asked Wild Animal Protection, an NGO in London, to help us. We managed to procure two captive bears and brought them here. Word spread, and soon we were receiving calls, letters, and emails from all over

Romania about other captive bears. We intervened and brought them here. Our bears Benny and Ali, for example, were kept for twenty-seven years in a concrete pen with iron bars. Now, they're here, free to roam. Some former owners visited, to see for themselves. They got it, finally, and that's what changed my mind."

"About?"

"Visitors, tourists. I realised you can only change people's mentalities through good example. I saw that our sanctuary could be a haven for bears *and* an educational resource for the public, especially children, like these, see?"

Cristina watches two young girls in matching red parkas. They stand transfixed as a bow-legged bear ambles from the edge of the forest, sniffing the ground.

"We have contracts with lots of schools, now, and I'm glad," says Cristina. "But my only real happiness is that I kept my promise to Maya."

We move on. Cristina takes her time, stepping carefully around potholes and loose rocks. She moves with determined grace, sure of her destination and how to get there.

The guide in the green top summons the girls to rejoin her group. She spots us and waves a hand. Cristina raises a thumb.

"That's Anca. Our guides accompany each group to provide information. For example, yesterday someone asked, *Why not just release the bears?* We explain that they would not survive. People ask, *How can you tell the bears apart?* We explain they're all microchipped for ID and medical checks, plus, they're our family, so we know who's who. Or, people will ask, *Can your bears breed?* So, we explain that we castrate all male bears because we don't want cubs in captivity. Things like that."

"You couldn't release the cubs as adults?" I ask.

"No, they would have no survival skills. If you feed a bear, just once, it is lost to the forest. A bear is an opportunistic animal and will come back for more because receiving food is easier than searching for it. A bear gets accustomed to freebies. To counteract this, we try to make their dinner time a natural activity. You'll see what I mean, in a little while, when the food wagon comes."

The tourists move up the trail to the next enclosure, where children point and laugh at something inside the high fence.

"Sounds like fun, shall we see?" says Cristina.

We join the tourists and watch two young bears playing in a big pool of water, chest deep. It's five or six metres in diametre. They tumble and splash, snarl and grunt, swishing away.

"Does every enclosure have a pool?" I ask.

"Of course. Water is very important to bears. They adore to swim, even in winter. You'll see them scratch the ice, break it, and go through. Our pools have flowing water and cannot become stagnant like in some zoos, but there are no fish here – I'm against fishing. Besides, these bears don't know how to fish and they get enough food from us."

One of the bears climbs out of the pond, but the other one grabs its hind leg. *No, stay and play!*

"Just like kids," Cristina says, with a chuckle. "They're from Albania, by the way."

"Do you have many bears from abroad?"

"Several. For example, I received a call from someone in America who worked at the SPCA – the Society for the Prevention of Cruelty to Animals – in Texas. A bear named Betty had been found in poor condition at a circus and they asked me if it could come here. I was quite surprised, but we agreed. Betty was in a bad state when she arrived and still is, but she gets along well with the other bears and seems happy enough, so, that's the main thing. We have bears from Georgia, and Armenia too."

"One big happy family?"

"That's the idea. I was asked recently, *Why do you accept bears from other countries?* My answer was, *Bears are simply bears.* Ours get along, regardless of where they're from. I don't know which of them learned to speak Romanian, or perhaps English, but they understand each other! This idea of nationalities, passports, and citizenship was invented by humans. I'll accept any bear who is in danger, they're welcome. Yes, our dominant males can be a bit territorial but it's not a big problem."

The metallic growl of an engine drifts through the forest, somewhere ahead of us, and Cristina says, "Food wagon. Watch this."

Bears climb backwards down tree trunks, clamber dripping wet from pools, and emerge from the forest. One by one, they lumber towards the fence, attracted by the sound of the engine, whose distant drone becomes a rattling roar, as it gets closer.

A pick-up truck painted in camouflage appears on the road and wobbles slowly past us, with big plastic containers stacked in the back. It disappears around a corner, pursued by a posse of bears small, medium, and large. One of them is almost as big as the truck.

"Obviously, they know it's dinner time," says Cristina, "but they don't know *where*, so they follow the truck. We vary our routine, throwing the food over the fence at different times and at different places each day. The bears have to come and search as they would in the wild. They'll spend hours foraging for sunflower seeds, or whatever. It gives them something to do, which is different to life in a zoo, where bears just wait until the keeper comes, once a day, at a set time, in the same place, and then they eat. Here, we try to let them live naturally. Best of all would be to take down the fences, of course, and let them go, but it's too late, they have lost their survival skills. They'd starve."

Cristina points upwards. "See these birds? Very intelligent. They follow the wagon, too."

The sky is blotched black with crows; hundreds of huge, flapping crows, whose wings seem to brush the treetops as they zoom above us, cackling, and cawing. A *murder* of crows, if you will.

"The bears will let them feed and don't seem to mind," says Cristina, with a chuckle. Nice to see her smile.

"Is it true," asks Angela, "that your sanctuary is one of the best in the world?"

Our host seems almost apologetic when she answers. "Well, yes, apparently so. There is an organisation, the European Alliance of Rescue Centres and Sanctuaries, or EARS, for short. They evaluate sanctuaries and told me we are among the seven best in the world – for any type of animal. People ask if I am *proud or happy*. I'm neither."

"Because you could make the sanctuary better?" I ask.

"It's not that, it's this: I'm not *happy*, firstly, because there are still bears in the world who are suffering.

Secondly, I'm not *proud,* because I would prefer this place not even to exist. You look surprised, but I'm serious. Even if our bears enjoy this five-star, all-inclusive whatever, I just wish there were no need for such a sanctuary and that all bears had remained in the forest where they belong."

"But, as you said, *they can't go back.* You gave them a fresh start, you don't feel proud or glad about that?"

"Glad, yes, proud no. Put yourself in the bear's position: when they enter this place and touch the electric wire for the first time, they get a shock and know they will never be free, not really, ever again. That troubles me, because freedom is a gift to us all when we are born, and nobody has a right to take an animal's freedom. Here, we just do our best to give some of it back. *Proud?* No, never."

We follow Cristina around the sloping bend to a wider lane flanked by tall trees. The bears are gathered in small groups inside the fence, nosing and munching at piles of food. One bear reclines on its haunches and looks like a big brown armchair you could snuggle in to read a book – *Goldilocks,* perhaps. The crows flit and flap across the grass, pecking at scraps. Several fly away with food in their long beaks.

The tourists are busy snapping photos. A few wander off to investigate a rusty steel cage, three metres long by two metres wide. The door is open and they step inside, one by one, grim-faced. Anca the guide remains outside and explains in a loud voice for the group to hear.

"This cage held a female bear for twelve years in Covasna. Her name was Odi. She was fed only corn. Look how malnourished she was."

Anca points to an information panel, where laminated photos show Odi the bear in the bad old days, when she was just fur and bones standing in this same cage, its floor a lattice of iron bars. In one shot, Odi stares, utterly miserable, at a heap of dried corn husks. The tourists emerge from the cage, in silence. One of the women is wiping her eyes.

Cristina beckons us. "You didn't see our chapel, yet."

She leads us to a lawn on a bluff overlooking the lane, with a small wooden chapel at the far end. We enter and peer at stained glass windows, one of which shows an elderly, bearded man dressed in a rough robe, outside a cave. He's feeding a bear.

"This is Saint Seraphim, the famous hermit," says Cristina. "Many saints befriended animals. Saint Ilie, Saint Isaac, the list goes on."

"How about Saint Francis?" I ask.

"Of course, he's here, too." Cristina points to another window. Sunlight catches the bright colours of Assisi and we bask in the glow of the righteous. Even so, my inner pagan has a question.

"Why a chapel, Cristina?"

"To remind visitors about these saints, and so we can invite priests to celebrate services on special days. It's about education, after all."

"Through religion?" says Angela.

"That's the idea, yes. I noticed priests never mentioned animals, in church, yet the Bible says God made animals as our companions."

"Fair point."

"There's more. The Bible also says we should be merciful. To my mind, that means mercy for animals too. So, I went to see an Orthodox priest and explained how the church could have a role in education here, because people would listen. I asked him to come and bless our bears. I've seen priests blessing cars, buildings, even missiles, so why not?"

"Did he agree to your request?"

"Of course, very helpful. We've had several priests here. It's nice, people seem to like it when a priest explains the connections."

"Between?"

"Everything. For example, do you know the origin of the word *animal?*"

I shake my head. Angela looks equally bemused. Roger smiles his patrician smile. He's heard this one before, probably.

"It's Latin," says Cristina, "it means *soul.*"

Heading back down the slope towards the main gate, Cristina points towards the high fence on our left. "There's Kira, shy as ever."

I'm expecting to see another bear, but instead, a small grey wolf trots through dense undergrowth, its tongue out and tail bushy.

"We rescued her, too. She lives with a couple of bears, they get along well. Wolves are social creatures, too. They need company."

Back at base, Cristina invites us for a quick peep at the small but impressive Bear Museum. We wander aisles of charming exhibits: two giant stuffed bears from outside Buckingham Palace, pictures painted by young visitors, and row after row of cute teddy bears donated by stars of stage and screen, including a teddy bear from Mr Bean.

Cristina shrugs. "Amazing, isn't it, all this? Do you know, teddy bears are still the most popular toys for young children, all over the world? Just about every kid has a bear, at some point, and it goes everywhere with them. So, here's a question for you: how is it that some people, when they grow up, become hunters and kill their dreams? Or become cruel and lock bears in a cage?"

There's no answer, and we move back outside, where special guests from around the world are enjoying a picnic, of sorts, on trestle tables. Turns out they're longstanding patrons who need a sit down. A jolly, rotund Englishwoman with hair the colour of beetroot tells us she makes teddy bears for a living and this is her fourth visit. I doubt it will be her last. We shake hands and move on.

In the security room, thirty-two video screens show the various enclosures, day and night. A pale-faced woman sits in front of them, observing closely. It looks like a scene from *Nature Watch.*

"Do you allow scientific study?" I ask.

Cristina frowns. "Absolutely not. Coffee?"

We sit at a long table in Cristina's office and she lights a cigarette. It's her sanctuary, after all. We sip good coffee and Cristina points to a striking, framed photo of a bear.

"There's Maya. Her story has a big effect on people who visit us, especially children when they watch our little film about her, in our reception area. Once, a weeping young boy said to me, *I want to see Maya, I want to give her flowers, where is she?* I crouched beside him and said, *Ask your father, on a clear night, to look in the sky and show you the biggest bear that exists – the Great Bear constellation. You'll see stars twinkling and know that Maya is up there, looking down, seeing happy bears, and now she is happy.* And do you know, that boy stopped weeping and said, *I shall protect bears and all the animals, always."*

"Nice story. That must make you glad, at least?"

"More than glad, Mike. It makes my life's work worthwhile. This is exactly what I want – to inspire visitors. I want them to remember Maya, that's all, because she was the reason for all this. Just remember Maya."

Author's note: For more information,
please visit *www.ampbears.ro*

Local Customs

"Package from China for you, Domnul Mike."

Our village postmistress rummages in her big canvas bag.

I watch and wait, rubbing my palms together.

"Excellent, Doamna Raluca, probably my scratch plate."

"Your what?"

"Just a bit of plastic for my guitar. I ordered it three months ago from Shanghai. I'd given up hope."

She gives me a little grey ticket. "Well, there you are."

"What's this?"

"It's a ticket." She fastens her bag and gets into her car.

"So, where's my scratch plate?"

"In Brașov, I suppose."

"Brașov?"

"At the Customs Office. You have to go there."

"You can't bring the package here?"

Our postmistress drives away, chuckling. *Silly Domnul.*

The drive to Brașov takes an hour and fifteen minutes and includes the inevitable near-death experience in pissing rain with an irresponsible driver coming the other way. Angela brakes hard. The black BMW roars past us and I glimpse a grinning dunce at the wheel, chatting on his phone.

We cruise around the city, looking for the Customs Office. We find it after twenty minutes or so, on a main road, which means we can't park outside unless we drive onto the pavement – illegal in theory and impossible in practice because dozens of cars are parked there already.

So, we drive around the back and are soon lost in a labyrinth of narrow streets flanked by apartment blocks painted in bright colours to match our darkening spirits. Eventually, Angela spies an empty place and reverses into it.

"I'll stay in the car," she says, "in case I'm parked in a dodgy spot."

Huddled under my umbrella, I scamper across puddles and through a dank, dark passage where the graffiti minces no words. It's the sort of place that even scallywags avoid, in case of scallywags.

"Ticket?" says the middle-aged clerk behind a high counter. Her spectacular hairstyle reminds me of something from *Dallas*. She's elbow deep in battered ledgers, their corners curled up like stale sandwiches. I hand over my ticket. She's chewing gum, lots of it. *Chew-chew.* She frowns at my ticket and I wonder why. Perhaps they've sent my package back, on a slow boat to China. Wouldn't surprise me, as two days have passed since I received the grey slip and these people don't muck about. *You had your chance.*

A man behind me in the queue decides, evidently, that he has a vital role to play in the proceedings and edges alongside me to watch. He flashes me a garlicky grin – *What's up?*

The clerk speaks from the side of her mouth. "Passport."

I hand mine over. She glances at the photo – *uh-huh* – and writes in a ledger. She runs her fingertip down a long column of inky scribble, cross-checking. It looks like tiresome work; her eyes must be killing her. Not to mention her jaw. *Chew-chew-chew.* Next time you're in a Post Office in Romania, count how many members of staff are chewing. For the purpose of this exercise, you may use your thumbs. Answers on a postcard, please, that will never arrive. But a little grey ticket might.

The clerk thrusts a pen at me. "Sign."

I sign.

She points. "Go over there."

I go over there.

This counter is lower but the stakes feel higher because the skinny woman behind it wears a shirt, tie, and a fitted jacket with impressive gold braid on the shoulders. Perhaps I've signed to join the Romanian navy. She slides a slim, padded envelope towards me.

"Please check the label. Is that your address?"

I look closer. The label has Chinese writing, here and there. *How exotic.* Makes sense, I suppose, if you're Chinese. Perhaps this is why *Poșta Română* couldn't deliver my package. Then again, my address is not in Chinese. It's in English. Right here, on the label. "Yup, correct, thanks."

The navy recruitment officer retrieves my envelope before I can get my mucky paws into it. "So what's inside, Domnul?"

"Just a bit of plastic."

"How much is it worth, in dollars?"

"Hmm, less than twenty, as far as I recall."

"What about this?" She points at the label. *Value $10*.

"Sounds about right," I say, wondering why she asked if she already knew.

"Now I have to open it, Domnul." She produces a glinting blade and slits the envelope's flap with a quick twist of her nimble wrist. She peeps inside, then nudges a form towards me.

"Customs release. Sign down there, then you can go."

I sign down there. She gives me the package and moves on to a pile of envelopes, turning them this way and that. Now I can go. And I would, if not for the troubling memory of how long it took me to get here, in wind and rain, and how, if not for Angela's quick reactions at the steering wheel, my wife and I would probably be Human Chow Mein, by now.

"Excuse me, Doamna, but I have a question."

"A question," she says, matter-of-factly. She doesn't look up.

"Yes, Doamna, why couldn't you deliver this to my house?"

She looks up. "Me?"

"Your colleagues in *Poșta Româna*, that is. I live far away, up in the mountains, which means a long drive for me, almost three hours, round trip. Couldn't you just send this to my house, or perhaps to our local post office so the postmistress could bring it?"

I wiggle the package. *Send this?* She watches it with nice blue eyes that do not blink.

"Domnul, *we* can't send it. This is the Customs Office, *Vama,* you see?" She points, with an envelope, towards a sign on the wall. VAMA.

"Yes, I know, Doamna, but I'm just asking why."

"Why what?"

"Why I have to come here."

"Because I'm a Customs Officer."

"Yes, but even so–"

"Even so?"

She'd make a good tennis player. *Whack, take that.*

"Doamna, you opened the envelope and asked me to sign. If that's all you have to do, couldn't our village postmistress do it?"

The customs officer tugs at her braided cuff and gives me a fierce look. *All I have to do?* She places her hands on her hips, elbows out. A psychologist might say she wants to make herself seem bigger. If so, it's working because I feel smaller by the second.

"Firstly, Domnul, China is not a member of Europe."

"I beg your pardon?"

"Secondly, China is therefore exempt from bilateral EU rules and agreements on postal services. Thirdly, your village postmistress is not a customs officer. That's why we must send you a ticket."

I wait for her fourthly and even her fifthly, but she's done. I think she just won. Game, set, and mailbox.

"Any more questions, Domnul?"

"No. Oh, actually, yes, just one. Next time I order something from China, should I send it to my family in England and ask them to post it to Romania? That way, the package will go straight to my door and I won't have to come here, is that correct?"

She mulls it over. "Correct, Domnul, at least for a while."

We smile, at last, and I'm glad. Nice to find common ground especially when you're right and they're wrong. Doamna leans across the desk for a quiet word. I can smell her perfume.

"There's just one problem, Domnul."

"I thought there might be."

"England is leaving Europe."

She wins, I lose. All because of Brexit. Little England just got even smaller. Or perhaps we're trying to make ourselves bigger, elbows out, like in the old days. We'll see.

"Hmm, so, eventually, I'll still have to come here?"

"Yes, Domnul, you will."

My blue-eyed, hard-working customs officer offers a sympathetic shrug. I reckon she's quite nice, once she's got you signed, sealed, and not delivered. In fact, she looks almost apologetic. I do like her smart uniform. I have a feeling that, as the plucky Brits sang during World War Two, *We'll meet again some, sunny day*. Unless it's raining cats and sheepdogs, of course, in which case, I might stay home.

Floating Voter

"Off to vote, Domnul Vasile?" I lean from the bedroom window, looking down towards our garden fence.

Our elderly neighbour pauses in the lane beyond it, and glances about with a puzzled smile, wondering where the voice came from. Despite the wintry weather, he's dressed dapper today – dark suit, shirt and tie, shiny shoes. His feet must be cold in all that snow and slush but he seems in good spirits, which is unusual, considering he probably hasn't got any spirits inside him just yet. Most of the time he wobbles along in an old tweed jacket, corduroys, and wellies caked in mud. Sometimes, he'll stop for a pee in the middle of the road and talk to himself. Or to Little Richard. But not today. He's going somewhere.

I wave a hand to catch his eye. "I'm up here, Vasile."

"Oh, it's you, Domnul Mike, *bună ziua.*" He points a stubby finger. "What's all this, nine o'clock and still in your pyjamas?"

"Late night, late start."

"Not me, Domnul Mike. I have to rise early. Sheep, see."

"And cows, eh?"

"Them, too." Vasile rests a hand on our fence. "You should get a couple of goats, Domnul Mike, this yard is plenty big enough."

"Goats? No chance. We've already got two dogs. And five cats, one of which is yours. She adopted us."

"Keep the damn cat. I never see her these days."

"So, are you going to vote?"

"Yes. It's a long walk in this, but I feel I should. And you?"

"I can't vote. I'm from England, a little country near Europe."

"So I hear." Vasile winks at me, sharp as ever.

I gesture towards foggy hills. "Important day for Romania, though, Domnul Vasile. So, I hope you'll vote for the right people."

"And who might they be?"

"People who'll make things better."

"Better what, Domnul Mike?"

"Better roads, schools, hospitals. And less corruption."

"In Romania? You must be dreaming. Go back to bed."

"I wish. Time to get up and work. So, who will you vote for?"

"Not the usual lot. What do they do for our village? We've got no bus, no gas, a dodgy water supply, and the snow plough hardly comes. And what about jobs, real jobs? My wife works in Germany for ten months a year just so we can renovate the house. Get my vote? They'll get my boot."

"Exactly, we need a change. So, who will you vote for?"

"No idea. I'll wait until I get there."

"Then what?"

"I'll look at the list, find a name I never heard of, and vote for them."

"Fingers crossed. How come you're not wearing gloves?"

"Who needs 'em? Not cold."

"I've got a thermometre up here. It says minus five Celsius."

"Better get dressed then, hadn't you? Bye."

Vasile pushes back from the fence, and moves on, stepping around gloopy puddles and adjusting his black astrakhan hat. I watch him go, and hope for warmer days. The sun is trying to penetrate the thick, grey fog that sits on our hills and fills our valleys. But the fog won't budge. It wants to stick around, engulf us, stop us seeing. Perfect weather for an election in Romania.

Yes Uke Can

Christmas Day, just before noon, we assemble outside our little village church, all dressed in our best. Twelve kids hand me their ukuleles, one by one, for tuning. My hands are cold and so are the strings. *Tricky.* Still, the Lord is with us, I hope.

Elderly parishioners dodder up the stone steps into the porch, giving us mystified looks. The kids mooch around in their skirts and bonnets, suits and bowties, chatting and giggling.

Mos Crăciun brought me a new phone, look!

Our instruments tuned, we enter the church in single file, following Angela. I'm carrying my music stand, too – an awkward but essential part of any performance; made of black steel, it matches the parishioners' black clothes.

In the porch, I catch a whiff of mothballs. And of livestock, too, because these farming folks tend their cows and sheep every day, just about – the milk flows and so life goes.

The church is packed and we spend five minutes slithering through the narthex and into the nave. A woman in a headscarf turns and spots us. It's Miruna, the councillor's wife. She smiles and beckons, *come.*

We inch forward, all fourteen of us, through the tight crowd, whispering apologies. *Scuzați-mă, mulțumesc.*

"Glad you could make it," whispers Miruna, as we edge up.

"Thanks for inviting us," murmurs Angela.

"Good idea, Miruna, these kids are thrilled." I add, quietly.

An elderly man in a baggy suit gives us the eye. *Hush.*

The bearded young priest is chanting away and the faithful are blessing themselves, ten to the dozen. A grim-faced fellow swings a brass pot to release puffs of aromatic incense. The kids clutch their ukuleles and gawp up at the painted dome where angels soar and podgy-faced cherubs pluck lyres. The youngest member of our troupe, little Dragoș is muttering numbers to himself, over and over, *One, two, three.* Perhaps he's counting the strings on the lyres. He's a bit of a cherub himself, actually: big eyes, button nose, and pursed lips. He comes to this church every Sunday, it seems. Impeccable manners, too, with Angela and me, but foul-mouthed when he's out and about, or so the other kids tell us. For the moment, Dragoș just stares in wonder at the elaborately-painted ceiling. He's as good as gold leaf. *One, two, three.* Perhaps he's practising the intro to our finale – *Jingle Bells.*

A choir pipes up, teenagers all. They're dressed in traditional peasant attire – embroidered smocks and dark skirts for the girls, white shirts and black waistcoats for the boys. They sing better than we will but their song is a dirge, and I can't help wonder. *Orthodox services seem unrelentingly solemn, how come?* I think back to Africa; attending church on the so-called Dark Continent was a bright, happy, thumping affair. Praise the Lord and whack that drum. Not that we went very often, only when we were invited. Like today. Nice to be asked, of course, but something doesn't seem right. Eventually, I realise: *the choir is looking towards the front; all we see are their backs. Why don't they face the people, instead?*

In fact, the only faces we see in here – apart from the priest's – are those of miserable-looking saints painted on cracked wooden alcoves. I suppose those cherubs look happy, overhead, but they're in paradise. Down here, I feel like I'm on Death Row and so would Father Christmas.

I whisper in Angela's ear. "I have a suggestion. When it's our turn to sing, we should face the audience."

"The congregation."

"Whatever, they should see our choir and vice versa."

"But in an Orthodox church, only the priest faces the people."

"Let's be unorthodox. If anyone complains later, blame me. Tell them I was raised Catholic. Besides, Miruna asked us *to sing carols for the people in church on Christmas Day.*"

"True."

"So, when it's time, we walk up there and turn around to face them. Tell the kids: smallest upfront, biggest at the back. Can we do that?"

"Yes, now be quiet."

The choir drones on for ten minutes. The priest stands with his hands across his tummy, gazing at the patterned carpet. He looks bored stiff. His job can't be easy, wearing those heavy brocade vestments and leading interminable services. Still, heaven awaits.

The dirge ends and it's our turn. Angela leads the way forward, whispering to the kids. They look puzzled. We gather together, facing the people, under a glittering chandelier that hangs from spindly chains; if they break, we'll be crowned for eternity.

I set my music stand where we can all see it, and open our songbook. We'll start with *Deschide Ușa, Creștine – Open The Door, Christians.* The rhythm, in swinging, waltzing 3/4 time, can be difficult for us to get right as a group, but the carol is popular and lively, and should brighten things up. I tap little Dragoș's shoulder. He's in pole position and I'd better remind him why.

"Remember to turn the pages in the songbook, Dragoș."

He glances up, gripping his ukulele. He looks apprehensive, as though we're about to ride in a roller coaster. I lean closer and whisper, "Don't worry, you'll do fine, we're all proud of you."

"Mulțumesc, Domnul Mike."

"Cu plăcere."

"Domnul Mike, shall I turn the page now?"

"Not yet. After each song. We'll do three, yes? Be ready."

"I'm ready."

"Good, don't forget."

"After each verse."

"Song."

"That's what I meant. I'm ready."

So is the congregation. Some people smile at us. Others seem taken aback by our effrontery. Happy are the parents, however, whose kids are in the ukulele group. Time to show 'em what we can do. We start with eight strums, then sing our hearts out.

> *Deschide ușa, creștine!*
> *Deschide ușa, creștine!*
> *Că venim și noi la tine!*
> *La mulți ani, mulți ani cu bine!*

The villagers sing along and the ancient rafters ring. The cherubs beam down and pluck their lyres. Angela catches my eye: *Mike, check the priest.* I turn to see. The priest is standing to one side, holding up his smartphone, and filming our little band of players. He notices that we're watching him, and nods in our direction: *Nice work!*

We finish our first carol and people clap their hands, which is surely a first in this Holy of Holies. So far, so good. Our opening song went well. Little Dragoș is bowing from the waist, up and down, like some child prodigy who wrote the damn thing. I lean through a gap behind him and whisper, "Dragoș, next page."

He grins up at me. "What?"

Author Bio

Mike Ormsby was born in Ormskirk, England. His short story collection, *Never Mind the Balkans, Here's Romania* (2008), prompted Romanian critics to dub him "our British Caragiale", after their beloved Victorian-era satirist.

Mike is the author of *Child Witch Kinshasa* and *Child Witch London* (2014), a two-part novel set in Congo and the UK. *Spinner the Winner* (2012), his book for children, has been translated into French, Serbian, Spanish and Romanian. His screenplay *Hey, Mr. DJ* (2007) was filmed in Kigali and shown at Rwanda's first Hillywood Film Festival.

A former BBC journalist/World Service trainer, Mike is based in a village in Transylvania, where he and his wife Angela Nicoară have lived for five hundred years.

DON'T MISS

MIKE ORMSBY'S
PALINCASHIRE — TALES OF TRANSYLVANIA

Italy has Tuscany, France the Loire, and Romania has Palincashire in beautiful Transylvania. Little known until now, Palincashire is located south of fact and east of fiction. In Palincashire, all your guidebooks come true, and if you believe that you'll believe anything.

Mike Ormsby returns to put Palincashire on the literary map. Join him in his adopted home!

Funny, moving, beautiful, and true to life.
Lucy Abel-Smith, Author, *Travels in Transylvania* Blue Guide

Affectionate, entertaining, and very funny.
Nick Hunt, Author, *Walking the Woods and the Water*

Humorous affection dusts every finely-honed phrase.
Douglas Williams, Editor, *OZB magazine*

Mike conjures scenes with a lovely light touch and distinctive humour.
Nigel Shakespear, Editor, *Times New Romanian*

Like 65 proof palinca offered at 10 a.m., these stories fill you with both happiness and sadness.
Raluca Feher, Author, *America dezgolită de la brâu în jos*

EXCERPT OVERLEAF

SAMPLE

PALINCASHIRE
TALES OF
TRANSYLVANIA

MIKE ORMSBY

The Magic Words

The elderly woman standing in the centre of Brașov has sad eyes and a big book: *The Brothers Grimm.* She looks about as hungry as the wolf on the cover. She offers the book to some passers-by, who pass but don't buy. She spots me approaching and says, "Mister, Mister, twenty lei."

Twenty lei. That's what, about five euros? I pause for a peep, flicking musty pages. It's a vintage hardback in Romanian with good illustrations, and she needs the cash. Her floral dress is washed out and an empty shopping bag dangles from her wrist. It's no fairy tale out here under this scorching summer sun.

"Call it fifteen lei, Mister, if you like."

I open my wallet and pay up. "Done."

"*Mulțumesc,* God bless."

She has good manners and I have *Hansel & Gretel.* Not to mention all the rest. I'll read some on the train home, improve my vocabulary. What's *gingerbread* in Romanian?

I hop on a bus for the station, gazing out at the cobbled lanes and tall, narrow houses with their solid beams and steep roofs. Like so much of Transylvania, this place offers tantalising hints of history.

The bus cruises around a slow bend and I gaze at the huge, steep, wooded hill overlooking the city. The Dacians dug a bone pit on that hill – evidence of a pagan cult, according to the archeologists – and, once upon an empire, somewhere up that slope, the Romans built a sacrificial altar dedicated to the god Tempus – their personification of *the moment* or *a convenient opportunity*. That's why, these days, that hill is called *Tâmpa*, although you should probably check, because times change and it might be called *Rolex* by now.

German colonists had their opportunity in the 12th century, when Hungarian kings invited them to build, mine and cultivate; they came, saw, and Saxonized this region, followed by the Teutonic Knights who founded the city during the Crusades, called it *Kronstadt,* and lost it when the Hungarians booted them out. Eventually, the communists turned up, whose genius, lest we forget, paved the way for McDonalds, Pizza Hut, and Starbucks. Three hundred years from now, perhaps little green men and lanky purple women will stroll through these narrow alleys with the thick walls and low arches, and wonder what was in our burgers. Interesting place, Brașov. Winter can be hard in the Carpathian Mountains, but, so far, this summer seems just right.

The station is as decrepit as ever, although the trains run on time, sometimes. *Platform 1 in 10 minutes* can mean *Platform 4 in 2 minutes,* and *A forty-minute delay* can mean *You should've brought your sleeping bag.* Assuming, of course, that you can fathom the travel updates bawled from tannoy speakers in this humungous hall of unintelligible echoes. It's like standing in a salt mine, where all you can find is pepper.

I doubt the ancient Romans would put up with it, if they were here. They'd sacrifice that travel announcer, on their altar, for telling whoppers. Then again, looking on the bright side, all this would probably make a good PR campaign: *Free Fairy Tale with Every Ticket.*

I buy mine from a large woman who lives in a small kiosk, then walk up pink marble stairs to the mezzanine – a good place to wait. I find an unbroken plastic seat, and sit. Dusty hikers trudge past. A middle-aged man in a Ceaușescu-era safari suit squints at the schedule. A pee-stained drunk lies face up, on a bench, mouth open. *What if one of these soaring pigeons plops in it?*

A pretty girl in a tatty yellow T-shirt trots towards me. She's about eight years old. Her jeans are too big and her long belt is looped twice around her concave tummy. She smiles, head tilted.

"Mister, give me money."

It seems this is my job and she's my boss. I smile back. "Hello there, and what are the magic words?"

"Huh?"

I explain about *please.* "The magic words are *vă rog.*"

"Vă rog, Mister."

I hand her two lei. "And afterwards?"

She grins, cute little beggar that she is. *"Vă rog,* Mister."

"No, *mulțumesc.*"

"Mulțumesc."

She skips away but soon returns, chewing a sticky bun as big as her head. She sits nearby, *munch munch,* smiling. She knows a sucker when she sees one. I'm an ATM on legs. She has big brown eyes. I glimpse a bright future in there and beckon her. *You, here, now.* She approaches with a wary gaze.

"What's your name, please?" I ask.

"Rushinta."

"I'm Mike. Can you read?"

"Sigur, domnu'!"

"Glad to hear it, this is for you."

I pull *The Brothers Grimm* from my bag and Rushinta's eyes pop when she clocks the dastardly wolf. "This is for me?"

"Yes, and I want to write your name inside. How do I spell it?" I dip in my bag for a pen.

Rushinta has other ideas. "Let me do it!" She sits alongside. "Big letters or small ones?"

"As you wish."

I give her the pen and she writes her name, slowly, in block capitals on the flyleaf. I scribble a dedication underneath and she grabs her prize. "Should I read this book now?"

"If you like, Rushinta."

She runs a finger across the first page, mouthing the words. After a few minutes, she looks up. "Ten lines already, Mister."

"Congratulations. Any good, that story?"

"Yes, but why did you give me this book?" Rushinta wrinkles her little nose at me. Strangers don't give you books. They give you money, or food, or nothing. I sit wondering. *Ah, I know.* I pull my keys from a pocket and select one at random. "This is a key to a door, Rushinta."

She looks at the key, then at me. "I know."

I point at her page. Her fingertip is poised, so I'd better be brief. "Rushinta, books are important. They are the key to your future, they will open doors in your life. Do you understand?"

"Sort of."

"Good, so read every day. You'll get smarter, every day, I promise. Do you promise?"

She sighs and looks a bit worried. *Every day?* Perhaps time is tight at home. "I'll try."

"Good, please do. Now, how are Hansel and Gretel doing?"

Rushinta reads aloud and I listen, watching pigeons soar. What were the chances, today, that I'd meet a tired old woman who needed money and an energetic little girl who needs something more? All I need now is a pigeon to plop in that drunk's gob. *Vă rog.*

I sit in my train, watching people shuffle along the platform with their bags and worried faces. A sweaty guard taps the steel wheels with a steel rod. Question is why.

A yellow blur rouses me. Rushinta zigzags between the travellers, begging here, pleading there. Most ignore her but some oblige with cash. She's not carrying the book. Perhaps she sold it. *Binned it?* She slithers through a group of hikers and vanishes from my sight. Never mind. I'll watch the sweaty guard.

Rushinta reappears soon enough, perched on a bench and kicking her heels. She doesn't see me. A whistle blows, wheels turn, and my train clanks away. I doubt we'll meet again. She'll forget our chat. Just another weird foreigner. One who can't help but watch and wonder from his seat.

Rushinta twists around, tugging at something tucked under her belt. She pulls the book free, lays it on her lap, and opens the cover. She turns the pages carefully and places a finger. Her little feet stop swinging as she reads the magic words.

Infectious Pizza

The cat flap flaps. A little furry head pokes through it, from the dark night beyond into our house. Bright green eyes glance left and right. Long whiskers sprout from the smudgy, black and white face. Freddie is not what you'd call a beautiful puss, but he's got something. Cattitude, that's what. *Here comes trouble.*

Tonight, he's also got something in his jaws: a tiny mouse alive and wriggling. But not for much longer, unless I intervene. Freddie realises that he's being watched and glares back at me with contracted pupils, two slits of suspicion. *Stay away, you.*

Some people might claim that a cat brings home a mouse as a gift for the master. *Really?* Try telling the cat.

Freddie scuttles under a chair and emits a strange noise, more growl than meow. I kneel and reach under.

"May I have that?"

Freddie makes another strange noise. *Fuck off.*

"Charming. Have you forgotten who rescued you?"

I never asked to be rescued.

"What if I drag you out, kitten mitten?"

You can try. Still mine.

"Actually, that mouse is a gift for me. Or so the experts say. You should read more, Fred."

You should mind your own business.

I tug our cat from his refuge and press my fingers gently at the hinge of his jaw. He drops the mouse. It darts under a rug. Freddie licks his pride and shoots me a glittering glance. *Thanks a lot.*

Now it's my turn to hunt, with an old spatula and a deep plastic box. Freddie watches with disdain. *Amateur.* But soon enough, the mouse scampers into the box, round and round, up and down, its tiny pink paws grappling in vain for traction. Seems in excellent shape too, considering its recent ordeal.

"There's a lucky rodent. Ye shall be released."

Freddie stares at me. *WTF?*

The mouse rises on its haunches, all whiskers and twitchy nose, to eye me up. I think we're bonding. It senses freedom is imminent, yay. I'm equally pleased. We're friends, now. I reach into the box, scoop up my cute little captive, and head for the door. A warm, evening breeze wafts in my face. Life is good.

The mouse jiggles in my hands. It needs air, perhaps. I open a gap between my interlocked thumbs and a grey head pokes though it. Tiny black eyes glisten, shiny as caviar. We observe each other – man and mouse – in wonder and mutual respect. Then it bites my thumb. *Take that.* I yelp in pain and drop the vicious little bastard, before it chews my arm off. Freddie rushes to reclaim his prize, flipping the mouse left and right. It is soon dazed, confused, and back in his jaws. Freddie slinks sway. *The End.*

I slump in a chair to inspect the damage. Fascinating stuff, blood. How it catches the light, shines ruby, regulates the life in us and scares the life out of us. My scarlet blob is growing bigger by the heartbeat. *What now?*

I'll probably bleed to death, home alone up this mountain. Or develop rabies and bounce off the walls at the sight of dishwater. What a way to go. I should probably write my will before my sacred ink runs out. Actually, I have a better idea. *Phone the vet.* He'll know what to do.

Cosmin takes my call but sounds weary – and who wouldn't – after a long day tending poorly animals. I explain that I have been most cruelly served by an ungrateful mouse. After a short silence, Cosmin says, "Mike, what are you, fucking nuts?"

In medical school, this is known as bedside manner, but then again, Cosmin didn't go there. He went to a school for veterinarians, if that's how you spell it.

We discuss the likelihood of my untimely demise from bubonic plague, and so on. It seems the risks are negligible but you never know. Cosmin asks when I last had a tetanus jab, but I never know. "I've had a yellow fever jab, Cosmin, is that any good?"

"Mike, don't you know anything?"

"If I drive down, can you give me a tetanus jab?"

"I'm a vet, not a doctor. You should go to Brașov and find the Hospital for Infectious Diseases."

"Oh, great, at this hour? Where is it, anyway?"

"In Brașov. Just ask for *Spitalul de Boli Infecțioase*. Write it down, in case you forget. Was it a mouse, or a baby rat?"

"I didn't ask. How does a baby rat look?"

"Like a rat."

"It was a mouse."

"Well, you should still go to the hospital."

Go to the hospital? I peer at my thumb. The bleeding has stopped. Perhaps I'll survive the night. Besides, *Brașov?*

"Cosmin, that's eighty kilometres. In the dark."
"You don't have headlights?"
"They're a bit wonky. Can I go tomorrow?"
"Up to you. Depends how long you want to live."
"Perhaps we should say goodbye."

So we do, and I reach for my car keys. Walking towards the door, I step on something tiny, furry, and dead. It's my bloody attacker, I'd know that face anywhere. Freddie sits nearby, licking his paws and doing the washing up – ears first, of course.

The dark and twisting forest road is dark and twisting even in daylight, but at night, with drunken headlights, it's enough to make you ratty. I could kill that rodent if it wasn't dead. Next time a cat brings me a present, I'll make popcorn. *Showtime.*

On we go. This rattling Suzuki jeep was modified for off-road shenanigans, but not by me. The drive takes an hour and by 11 p.m., I spy the twinkling, ancient city of Brașov. Sleeker cars zoom past me, containing lucky people who'll live long and happy lives if they slow down. Where are they off to, at this ungodly hour? Shouldn't they be home watching shite on Romanian TV? Look at them go, probably got Sat Nav, as well, whereas I have a scrap of paper bearing feverish scrawl – *Boli Infecțioase.* Infectious Diseases. *I've probably got one.* I need the hospital and soon. I hope it's open. Damn that mouse. I'd better get better directions if I want to get better. Time is slipping away.

I park outside an all-night pharmacy, pop inside, and explain that I've been bitten by a huge rat with teeth like this – *NEH-NEH-NEH* – and that I need the wotsit hospital. A handsome lady in a lab coat points up the street: *left, right, left again.* Her silver-haired male colleague peeps from a room behind her and looks me up and down. The fever is kicking in. He can tell.

After fifteen minutes of driving in circles, triangles, and rectangles, I realise I'm lost, literally and metaphorically. Not to mention scientifically, since I'll surely be dead by dawn. But how come? I've asked three people thus far, so either I'm hallucinating or they gave me dicky directions. *Ah, look, some zombies at a bus stop; one of them will know.* I park nearby and stride back to ask my question, but I've forgotten how to say *hospital*. Hmm, I'll say it like the French and omit the <s> in the middle: *hopital.* That should do it. The people at the bus stop turn to listen, as I approach and ask:

"Hôpital de boli infecțioase, vă rog?"

They seem a bit lost, which makes six of us.

"Domnul," says the woman nearest, "we don't live round here. Try that driver in the pizza van."

She points and I turn. Great idea. The pizza man is sitting with his window rolled down, fiddling with his keys. He starts the car, just as I glide up.

"Hôpital de boli infecțioase, vă rog?"

He raises bushy eyebrows. "*What* kind of pizza?"

We stare at each other in mutual wonder, but not much respect. He drives off before I can ask again. I have a feeling that something got lost in translation. Me, actually. None the wiser, I slink back to my car, raising a throbbing thumb at the bus queue. *All sorted, cheers.*

Eventually, I find the hospital – a small, nondescript building behind tall trees in a quiet street. No neon, no gates, no nothing, really. Blink and you'd miss it. Even so, I'm blinking relieved to be here.

The helpful young doctor listens carefully and summons a nurse, who prepares an injection and asks what sort of rodent bit me. I pull a transparent plastic zip-lock bag from my pocket. "This sort."

The nurse takes a step back. "Is that a mouse?"

"Hope so. It's dead, don't worry. Freddie killed it. He's my cat."

The doctor asks me to put the bag on a bench, out of harm's way. He sticks the needle in my arm and offers advice about what to do next time Freddie catches a mouse. Or rather, what not to do. His pager beeps, he bids me farewell and departs.

The nurse puts a little plaster on my arm. "You should be fine, but if not, just phone. Will that be all, or is there anything else, Domnul?"

Her perfume smells of roses and she has a lovely, reassuring smile. I do like nurses and rather wish I was a bit more sick. Oh, well. No, wait, I know.

"Actually, Nurse, please could you tell me how to pronounce the name of this place, in Romanian?"

"*Spitalul de Boli Infecțioase.*" She sounds proud, probably because it sounds so impressive, unlike whenever I say it. No wonder I got lost. But now I'm found. I will drive through the valley of darkness, with wonky headlights, fearing no evil.

"You've been very helpful, Nurse, *mulțumesc și la revedere.*"

"Don't forget your mouse," she says, pointing to the little plastic bag.

Palincashire – Tales of Transylvania
is available on Amazon